Green Innovation for a Sustainable Future: Harnessing Renewable Energy, AI, Blockchain, and Green Technologies for Environmental Transformation

Copyright

Green Innovation for a Sustainable Future: Harnessing Renewable Energy, AI, Blockchain, and Green Technologies for Environmental Transformation

ISBN 978-1-991369-11-6 (eBook)

ISBN 978-1-991369-12-3 (Paperback)

The information in this book is for general informational purposes only. The publisher and author make no representations or warranties regarding the accuracy, applicability, or completeness of the contents. The reader is encouraged to consult relevant professionals before making decisions based on the material in this book.

Table of Contents

Preface

The global urgency to transition toward a sustainable future has never been greater. With climate change, resource depletion, and environmental degradation threatening ecosystems and economies alike, the need for innovative solutions is paramount. In response, green innovation has emerged as a powerful force, leveraging cutting-edge technologies to drive sustainability and resilience.

This book explores the transformative role of renewable energy, artificial intelligence, blockchain, and green technologies in shaping a sustainable future. These advancements are not merely technological breakthroughs but fundamental shifts in how we generate energy, manage resources, and build societies. The integration of digital solutions with environmental strategies is redefining industries, enabling businesses, governments, and communities to reduce their ecological footprints while fostering economic growth.

As the world moves toward net-zero emissions and circular economies, the insights within this book offer a roadmap for harnessing innovation to address environmental challenges. By understanding the synergies between technology and sustainability, we can unlock new opportunities to mitigate climate risks, enhance efficiency, and create a resilient future for generations to come.

This book is a call to action for policymakers, business leaders, researchers, and individuals alike to embrace green innovation as a cornerstone of sustainable development. The solutions exist—now is the time to implement them.

Chapter 1: Introduction to Green Innovation

Green innovation lies at the heart of the global shift toward sustainability, offering transformative solutions to pressing environmental challenges. This chapter provides a foundational understanding of green innovation, exploring its definition, significance, and role in shaping a sustainable future. By examining the drivers behind this movement—ranging from policy and regulation to market demands—it highlights the interconnected factors propelling technological advancements. Additionally, the chapter delves into current global trends, offering insights into how green innovation is addressing critical challenges and paving the way for a more sustainable world. This exploration sets the stage for the in-depth analysis of specific technologies and their applications in subsequent chapters.

Understanding Green Innovation

Green innovation refers to the development and application of technologies, processes, and practices that promote environmental sustainability while driving economic and social progress.

Definition and Importance of Green Innovation

Green innovation encompasses the creation and implementation of new technologies, processes, and solutions that address environmental challenges while fostering economic growth and social well-being. At its core, green innovation seeks to reduce environmental impact, enhance resource efficiency, and contribute to the transition toward a sustainable future. This concept goes beyond merely addressing ecological concerns; it integrates sustainability into the fabric of innovation, making it a central driver of change across industries.

The importance of green innovation cannot be overstated in today's world. As climate change, biodiversity loss, and resource depletion intensify, traditional approaches to development and growth are proving inadequate. Green innovation offers a pathway to decouple economic progress from environmental degradation, ensuring that growth does not come at the expense of planetary health. By fostering the adoption of renewable energy, sustainable agriculture, and efficient manufacturing processes, green innovation helps mitigate greenhouse gas emissions and conserve natural resources.

Moreover, green innovation has a ripple effect across economies and societies. It drives job creation in emerging industries such as renewable energy, green manufacturing, and eco-friendly technologies. It also enhances corporate competitiveness by aligning businesses with the growing demand for sustainable products and practices. Governments and international organizations are increasingly prioritizing green innovation in policy frameworks and funding initiatives, further underscoring its critical role in achieving global sustainability goals.

In summary, green innovation is not just an option but a necessity for addressing today's environmental challenges while ensuring economic and social progress for future generations.

The Intersection of Technology and Sustainability

The intersection of technology and sustainability represents a transformative shift in how societies address environmental challenges while fostering economic growth. Technology serves as a powerful enabler of sustainable practices, offering innovative tools and solutions that improve efficiency, reduce resource consumption, and mitigate environmental harm. This convergence is evident across various sectors, where advancements in technology drive the adoption of sustainable practices at scale.

In energy, technologies such as solar panels, wind turbines, and energy storage systems are revolutionizing the way power is generated and consumed. These innovations not only reduce dependence on fossil fuels but also enable decentralized energy systems that enhance resilience and accessibility. Similarly, in agriculture, technologies like precision farming and AI-driven monitoring systems optimize resource use, minimize waste, and boost productivity, ensuring food security while reducing environmental impact.

Manufacturing industries are also leveraging technological advancements to adopt sustainable practices. Innovations such as 3D printing, automation, and machine learning enable more efficient production processes, reducing waste and energy use. Blockchain technology is increasingly being utilized to enhance supply chain transparency, ensuring that materials are sourced ethically and sustainably.

Additionally, digital technologies play a vital role in monitoring and addressing environmental issues. Satellite imaging, IoT devices, and big data analytics provide real-time insights into climate patterns, deforestation rates, and pollution levels, empowering policymakers and organizations to make informed decisions.

This intersection between technology and sustainability underscores the potential for innovation to drive significant progress toward a greener, more sustainable future. It highlights the critical role technology plays in enabling societies to address environmental challenges while achieving economic and social goals.

Drivers of Green Innovation

The drivers of green innovation are the diverse forces propelling the development and adoption of sustainable technologies and practices across industries.

Policy and Regulation

Policy and regulation play a pivotal role in driving green innovation by creating a framework that incentivizes sustainable practices and technological advancements. Governments and international organizations use policies and regulatory mechanisms to guide industries, businesses, and individuals toward adopting environmentally conscious behaviors and innovations. These measures set the groundwork for systemic change by aligning economic activities with environmental goals.

One of the primary tools governments use to drive green innovation is environmental legislation. Laws targeting carbon emissions, waste management, and resource conservation compel industries to seek innovative solutions to comply with legal requirements. For example, emission reduction mandates push businesses to invest in renewable energy technologies, while waste reduction policies encourage the development of circular economy practices. Regulatory frameworks such as these not only ensure compliance but also stimulate competition to create cost-effective and sustainable solutions.

Economic incentives also play a significant role. Subsidies, tax credits, and grants for green technologies lower the financial barriers to innovation. These incentives make it more viable for businesses and startups to invest in research and development, accelerating the commercialization of sustainable solutions. Renewable energy projects, for instance, benefit significantly from government-backed financial support, driving their rapid adoption globally.

Moreover, international agreements such as the Paris Agreement emphasize the role of collaborative policies in fostering green innovation. These agreements create a shared vision for sustainability, encouraging nations to adopt policies that support clean technologies and environmental conservation. They also provide platforms for knowledge sharing, enabling the global dissemination of best practices and innovations.

Policy and regulation also encourage accountability through mechanisms such as carbon pricing and emissions trading systems. By assigning a cost to environmental impact, these tools incentivize businesses to minimize emissions and adopt greener practices. Carbon pricing, in particular, has been instrumental in driving investments in renewable energy and energy efficiency technologies.

Additionally, standards and certifications play a critical role in shaping green innovation. These measures establish benchmarks for sustainable practices, enabling consumers and businesses to make informed choices. For instance, energy efficiency standards for appliances and buildings have driven technological advancements that reduce energy consumption and environmental impact. Similarly, certifications for sustainable products promote innovation in manufacturing processes and material use.

However, effective policy and regulation require a balance between ambition and feasibility. Overly stringent regulations can stifle innovation by imposing excessive costs, while weak policies may fail to incentivize meaningful change. Policymakers must also account for the varying capacities of industries and nations, ensuring that regulations are inclusive and adaptable.

Market Demand for Sustainable Practices

Market demand for sustainable practices has become a significant driver of green innovation, as consumers, businesses, and investors increasingly prioritize environmental responsibility. This growing demand stems from heightened awareness of climate change, resource scarcity, and the need for more sustainable lifestyles. As a result, companies are compelled to innovate, adopting and creating environmentally friendly technologies, processes, and products to meet the expectations of an eco-conscious market.

Consumer behavior has undergone a profound shift in recent years, with more individuals seeking products and services that align with their values of sustainability. Consumers are not only looking for eco-friendly options but are also demanding transparency in how goods are sourced, produced, and distributed. This shift has pushed businesses to adopt green supply chain practices, develop sustainable packaging, and reduce their overall environmental footprint. Green certifications and labels, such as organic or carbon-neutral designations, have gained importance as they influence purchasing decisions and build trust with customers.

Corporate clients are also driving demand for sustainable practices. Businesses increasingly evaluate their suppliers and partners based on sustainability criteria, recognizing the competitive advantage of aligning with environmentally responsible organizations. Companies that fail to meet these expectations risk losing contracts and damaging their reputation. This has encouraged innovation in areas such as energy efficiency, waste reduction, and sustainable resource management to ensure compliance with client demands.

The financial sector has also played a critical role in fueling market demand for sustainability. Investors are channeling capital into companies that demonstrate strong environmental, social, and governance (ESG) performance. Green bonds and sustainable investment funds are gaining traction, reflecting a preference for financing projects and businesses that contribute to environmental objectives. This focus on sustainability as a key investment criterion has incentivized companies to innovate, ensuring their operations and products align with investor expectations.

In addition to direct consumer and investor pressure, regulatory compliance tied to market demands has influenced the adoption of sustainable practices. Governments and organizations often set environmental standards that industries must meet, further driving innovation. For example, emissions regulations, waste disposal requirements, and energy efficiency targets encourage businesses to explore sustainable solutions to maintain market access and avoid penalties.

Technological advancements have enabled companies to respond to market demand for sustainable practices more effectively. Tools such as artificial intelligence and blockchain provide transparency and efficiency, allowing businesses to track their sustainability metrics and share verified information with stakeholders. Digital platforms have also amplified consumer voices, enabling them to advocate for sustainability and hold companies accountable.

Finally, the competitive landscape has shifted, with sustainability becoming a key differentiator for brands. Companies that lead in green innovation gain customer loyalty, attract top talent, and improve their market position. This has created a race among businesses to adopt sustainable practices and pioneer new solutions to environmental challenges.

Global Trends in Sustainability

Global trends in sustainability reflect a growing global commitment to addressing environmental challenges through innovative practices, policies, and technologies.

Current Global Environmental Challenges

The world is facing a multitude of environmental challenges that threaten ecosystems, economies, and human well-being. These challenges, driven by human activities and natural processes, are accelerating at an unprecedented rate, necessitating urgent and coordinated action to mitigate their impacts.

One of the most pressing issues is climate change, caused by the accumulation of greenhouse gases in the atmosphere due to the burning of fossil fuels, deforestation, and industrial activities. Rising global temperatures have led to more frequent and severe heatwaves, droughts, wildfires, and hurricanes. Melting polar ice caps and glaciers are contributing to sea level rise, threatening coastal communities and ecosystems. The disruption of weather patterns has significant implications for agriculture, water availability, and biodiversity, making climate change one of the foremost environmental challenges of our time.

Biodiversity loss is another critical issue. Habitat destruction, overexploitation of natural resources, pollution, and the introduction of invasive species have led to an alarming decline in plant and animal populations worldwide. According to studies, the current rate of species extinction is significantly higher than the natural background rate, jeopardizing ecosystem services such as pollination, water purification, and climate regulation that are essential for human survival.

Pollution, in various forms, continues to pose a significant threat to the environment and human health. Air pollution from industrial emissions, transportation, and energy production is a major contributor to respiratory diseases and premature deaths globally. Plastic pollution has reached alarming levels, with millions of tons of waste entering oceans each year, harming marine life and entering the food chain. Water pollution from agricultural runoff, industrial discharges, and untreated sewage further degrades freshwater ecosystems and affects the availability of clean water for communities.

Deforestation and land degradation are also significant challenges. Large-scale deforestation for agriculture, logging, and urban expansion results in the loss of critical carbon sinks, further exacerbating climate change. Soil erosion, desertification, and the depletion of arable land threaten food security, particularly in regions already vulnerable to hunger and poverty. The destruction of forests also disrupts the livelihoods of indigenous communities and contributes to the loss of biodiversity.

Water scarcity is emerging as a critical issue due to growing demand, inefficient water use, and the impacts of climate change. Over two billion people currently live in water-stressed regions, and this number is expected to rise as populations grow and water resources become increasingly strained. The competition for water between agriculture, industry, and domestic use poses challenges for equitable and sustainable water management.

Ocean degradation, driven by overfishing, pollution, and climate change, is another pressing concern. Rising sea temperatures and acidification disrupt marine ecosystems, threatening coral reefs, fisheries, and coastal livelihoods. Unsustainable fishing practices further deplete fish stocks, jeopardizing food security for millions of people who depend on seafood as a primary protein source.

These global environmental challenges are interconnected and require holistic and innovative approaches to address them effectively. The urgency to act has never been greater, as the consequences of inaction will profoundly impact future generations and the planet's ability to sustain life.

Emerging Trends in Green Innovation

Green innovation is evolving rapidly, driven by the urgent need to address environmental challenges and transition to a sustainable future. Emerging trends in green innovation are reshaping industries and creating new opportunities for achieving environmental, economic, and social goals through advanced technologies and practices.

One prominent trend is the integration of renewable energy technologies into mainstream energy systems. Innovations in solar, wind, and hydropower are making renewable energy more accessible, efficient, and cost-effective. Breakthroughs in energy storage, such as advanced lithium-ion batteries and next-generation solid-state batteries, are addressing the intermittency of renewable energy sources, enabling their widespread adoption. Microgrids and decentralized energy systems are also gaining traction, providing resilient and localized energy solutions for communities.

The rise of circular economy practices is another significant trend in green innovation. Companies are shifting from linear models of production and consumption to circular systems that prioritize resource efficiency and waste reduction. Innovations in recycling technologies, material science, and product design are enabling the recovery and reuse of materials, minimizing environmental impact. Industries such as fashion, electronics, and construction are increasingly adopting circular approaches, driving the demand for sustainable materials and closed-loop supply chains.

Digital technologies are playing a transformative role in advancing green innovation. Artificial intelligence (AI), blockchain, and the Internet of Things (IoT) are enabling real-time monitoring, predictive analytics, and transparency in sustainability efforts. AI is being used to optimize energy use, enhance precision agriculture, and manage natural resources more efficiently. Blockchain technology is revolutionizing supply chain management by ensuring traceability and accountability, while IoT devices provide valuable data for monitoring environmental conditions and improving efficiency in resource management.

Sustainable transportation is an area experiencing significant innovation. The electrification of vehicles, including cars, buses, and trucks, is reducing greenhouse gas emissions and air pollution in urban areas. Advances in battery technology, coupled with the expansion of charging infrastructure, are making electric vehicles (EVs) more practical and affordable. Additionally, innovations in sustainable aviation, such as hydrogen-powered aircraft and biofuels, are addressing emissions from air travel. Shared mobility solutions, such as ride-sharing and electric scooters, are also contributing to greener transportation systems.

Green building technologies are emerging as a key focus area for sustainability. Innovations in energy-efficient building materials, smart systems for energy management, and net-zero building designs are transforming the construction industry. The use of renewable energy sources, sustainable insulation, and intelligent lighting systems are helping to create buildings with lower environmental footprints. These advancements are being integrated into urban planning to develop sustainable cities and communities.

Hydrogen energy is also emerging as a versatile and sustainable solution for decarbonizing various sectors. Green hydrogen, produced using renewable energy, is being explored for applications in industry, transportation, and energy storage. As production costs decline, hydrogen is expected to play a significant role in the transition to a low-carbon economy.

These emerging trends in green innovation reflect a growing commitment to leveraging technology and creativity to address environmental challenges and build a more sustainable future. They are shaping industries and paving the way for transformative solutions that balance economic growth with ecological stewardship.

Chapter 2: Renewable Energy Innovations

Renewable energy innovations are at the forefront of the global transition to sustainable energy systems, offering solutions to reduce greenhouse gas emissions, enhance energy security, and address the growing demand for clean power. This chapter explores the transformative advancements in renewable energy technologies, focusing on solar, wind, and energy storage systems. It also examines decentralized energy systems, the role of policy and investment in driving these innovations, and the potential for these technologies to reshape energy systems globally. Through these explorations, this chapter highlights the critical role renewable energy plays in mitigating climate change and building a sustainable future.

Transforming Energy Systems

The transformation of energy systems is central to achieving a sustainable future, driven by the shift from fossil fuels to cleaner, renewable energy sources.

Transition from Fossil Fuels to Renewables

The transition from fossil fuels to renewable energy is a critical step in addressing climate change and achieving sustainable energy systems. Fossil fuels, including coal, oil, and natural gas, have historically been the dominant sources of global energy, powering industries, transportation, and households. However, their combustion releases significant amounts of greenhouse gases into the atmosphere, contributing to global warming and environmental degradation. The shift to renewable energy sources is driven by the need to mitigate these impacts while ensuring energy security and economic growth.

Renewable energy sources such as solar, wind, hydropower, and geothermal offer a sustainable alternative to fossil fuels. They are abundant, naturally replenishing, and emit little to no greenhouse gases during operation. Solar and wind power, in particular, have experienced rapid technological advancements, leading to significant cost reductions and increased efficiency. These developments have made renewables more competitive with fossil fuels in many regions, accelerating their adoption.

Governments, businesses, and international organizations are playing a pivotal role in this transition by setting ambitious renewable energy targets, implementing supportive policies, and investing in research and infrastructure. Innovations in energy storage, such as advanced batteries, are addressing the intermittency challenges of renewables, ensuring reliable and stable power supply.

The transition is also creating economic opportunities, from job creation in renewable energy sectors to the development of sustainable industries. While challenges remain, such as upgrading existing energy grids and managing the decline of fossil fuel industries, the shift to renewables represents a transformative change in the global energy landscape.

Decentralized Energy Systems

Decentralized energy systems represent a significant shift from traditional centralized energy generation, where power is produced at large facilities and transmitted over long distances to consumers. In decentralized systems, energy generation occurs closer to the point of consumption, often through renewable energy sources such as solar panels, wind turbines, and small-scale hydroelectric plants. These systems are transforming how energy is produced, distributed, and managed, offering numerous environmental, economic, and social benefits.

One of the key advantages of decentralized energy systems is their ability to enhance energy resilience. By distributing power generation across multiple locations, these systems reduce the risk of widespread outages caused by natural disasters, equipment failures, or cyberattacks. Localized energy production also minimizes transmission losses, improving overall efficiency and reducing the environmental footprint of energy distribution.

Decentralized systems empower communities and individuals to take control of their energy needs. Through technologies like rooftop solar panels, small wind turbines, and microgrids, consumers can generate their own power, reduce dependency on centralized utilities, and potentially sell excess energy back to the grid. This democratization of energy supports energy independence and fosters innovation in localized energy solutions.

Advancements in digital technologies, such as smart grids and blockchain, are further enabling the growth of decentralized energy systems. These tools facilitate real-time energy management, peer-to-peer energy trading, and seamless integration of renewable sources. As decentralized energy systems continue to expand, they are playing a crucial role in the transition to a more sustainable, equitable, and efficient energy future.

Advances in Solar and Wind Technologies

Advances in solar and wind technologies are revolutionizing renewable energy, making these sources more efficient, affordable, and accessible than ever before.

Next-Generation Solar Panels

Next-generation solar panels are pushing the boundaries of efficiency, durability, and versatility, driving the widespread adoption of solar energy across residential, commercial, and industrial sectors. Traditional silicon-based photovoltaic (PV) panels have dominated the market for decades, but advancements in materials and manufacturing techniques are enabling the development of new solar technologies with enhanced performance and broader applications.

One of the most promising advancements in solar technology is the emergence of perovskite solar cells. Perovskite materials have demonstrated remarkable efficiency improvements in converting sunlight into electricity, rivaling and even surpassing traditional silicon-based cells. These materials are also less expensive to produce, as they require lower energy inputs during manufacturing. Additionally, perovskite solar cells are lightweight and flexible, opening new possibilities for integration into building materials, vehicles, and portable devices.

Bifacial solar panels represent another innovation in solar technology. Unlike conventional panels that capture sunlight on one side, bifacial panels are designed to absorb light on both sides, utilizing reflected sunlight from surfaces such as the ground or rooftops. This design increases overall energy generation, making bifacial panels particularly effective in installations with high reflectivity, such as snowy or sandy environments.

Thin-film solar technologies are also gaining attention for their unique advantages. These panels use materials like cadmium telluride or copper indium gallium selenide to create ultra-thin, lightweight solar cells. Thin-film panels are highly adaptable and can be integrated into a wide range of surfaces, including windows, facades, and curved structures. Their flexibility and lightweight nature make them ideal for applications where traditional panels are impractical.

Another breakthrough in solar panel technology is the development of tandem solar cells. These cells combine multiple layers of different materials to capture a broader spectrum of sunlight, significantly increasing efficiency. Tandem solar cells are particularly valuable for applications where space is limited, such as urban rooftops or solar-powered vehicles.

Durability and longevity are also key focuses in next-generation solar panel development. Innovations in coatings and materials are improving resistance to extreme weather conditions, temperature fluctuations, and degradation from UV exposure. This enhances the lifespan of solar panels, reducing maintenance costs and improving the return on investment for solar energy systems.

In addition to efficiency and durability, researchers are exploring new ways to improve the aesthetic appeal of solar panels. Transparent and semi-transparent solar panels are being developed for use in windows and facades, allowing buildings to generate electricity without compromising design. Similarly, customizable colors and patterns are being introduced to make solar panels blend seamlessly with architectural styles.

These advancements in next-generation solar panels are not only increasing the efficiency and versatility of solar energy systems but also expanding their applications across diverse industries and environments. As costs continue to decline and technologies mature, next-generation solar panels are poised to play a pivotal role in accelerating the transition to a clean and sustainable energy future.

Offshore Wind Innovations

Offshore wind innovations are transforming the renewable energy landscape by harnessing the vast wind resources available over open waters. With stronger and more consistent wind speeds than onshore sites, offshore wind farms have the potential to generate significant amounts of clean energy. Recent technological advancements are driving improvements in efficiency, scalability, and cost-effectiveness, making offshore wind a cornerstone of the global energy transition.

One of the most notable innovations in offshore wind technology is the development of larger and more efficient wind turbines. Turbines with capacities exceeding 15 megawatts (MW) are being deployed, allowing each unit to generate more power and reduce the number of turbines required for a project. These larger turbines are equipped with advanced blade designs, which maximize energy capture even in low wind conditions. Innovations in materials, such as lightweight composites, enhance the durability and performance of these turbines in harsh marine environments.

Floating wind farms are another groundbreaking development in offshore wind energy. Unlike traditional fixed-bottom turbines, which are anchored to the seabed, floating turbines are mounted on buoyant platforms that can be deployed in deeper waters. This technology expands the potential for offshore wind development to areas where fixed-bottom installations are not feasible, significantly increasing the global capacity for wind energy. Floating wind farms also minimize environmental impacts on seabed ecosystems and provide greater flexibility in site selection.

Digital technologies are playing a critical role in optimizing offshore wind operations. Advanced sensors and data analytics enable real-time monitoring of turbine performance, weather conditions, and maintenance needs. Predictive maintenance systems use AI to identify potential issues before they cause downtime, reducing operational costs and enhancing reliability. Drone inspections are becoming a common practice, allowing for efficient and safe assessment of turbines in challenging offshore environments.

Grid integration is another area of innovation in offshore wind energy. High-voltage direct current (HVDC) transmission systems are being used to transport electricity from offshore wind farms to onshore grids with minimal energy losses. These systems are particularly effective for long-distance transmission, making them ideal for large-scale offshore projects. Additionally, efforts are underway to develop offshore energy hubs, where multiple wind farms can connect to a central platform for efficient power transmission and storage.

Environmental considerations are also driving innovations in offshore wind technology. Turbine designs are being adapted to minimize their impact on marine life, such as incorporating features that deter birds from flying into blades. Noise reduction technologies are being developed to lessen the impact of construction and operation on marine mammals. Environmental monitoring systems are also being integrated into wind farms to assess and mitigate ecological impacts.

The combination of technological advancements, digital tools, and environmental stewardship is propelling offshore wind energy to new heights. These innovations are making offshore wind more accessible, efficient, and sustainable, solidifying its role as a critical component of the global renewable energy portfolio. As investments and research continue, offshore wind innovations are poised to unlock even greater potential for clean energy generation.

Integrating Renewables into the Grid

Integrating renewable energy into existing power grids is a critical challenge and opportunity in the global transition to clean energy. The intermittent nature of renewable sources, such as solar and wind, requires innovative technologies and strategies to ensure a stable, reliable, and efficient electricity supply. Addressing these complexities involves advancements in grid infrastructure, energy storage, and smart grid technologies.

One of the primary challenges in integrating renewables is their variability. Solar energy production depends on sunlight, and wind energy fluctuates with wind speed, leading to periods of overproduction or undersupply. To address this, grid operators are adopting flexible energy systems capable of managing fluctuations. Demand response programs, for instance, allow utilities to adjust energy consumption during peak times, helping to balance supply and demand.

Energy storage systems play a pivotal role in smoothing out the variability of renewables. Advanced battery technologies, such as lithium-ion, flow, and solid-state batteries, store excess energy generated during periods of high renewable output. This stored energy can then be dispatched during times of low production, ensuring a consistent energy supply. Pumped hydro storage and emerging technologies like hydrogen storage further expand the options for grid-scale energy storage.

Grid modernization is another critical aspect of integrating renewables. Upgrading transmission and distribution infrastructure is essential to accommodate the increased share of renewable energy. HVDC systems enable efficient long-distance transmission of electricity from renewable energy sources, such as offshore wind farms or solar arrays in remote areas, to urban centers. Additionally, enhancing grid interconnectivity allows energy to flow between regions, optimizing the use of renewable resources across wider areas.

Smart grid technologies are revolutionizing the way energy is managed and distributed. Equipped with sensors, communication systems, and automation tools, smart grids provide real-time data on energy production, consumption, and grid conditions. This data enables operators to make informed decisions, such as rerouting power, integrating distributed energy resources, and identifying faults quickly. AI and machine learning are increasingly being employed to predict energy demand and optimize grid performance.

Decentralized energy systems, including microgrids, are also facilitating the integration of renewables into the grid. Microgrids operate semi-independently from the main grid, using local renewable energy sources like solar panels or wind turbines to provide power to communities or facilities. These systems enhance grid resilience, particularly during outages, while promoting the use of clean energy at a local level.

Policy and regulatory frameworks play an essential role in enabling renewable integration. Incentives for grid modernization, support for energy storage development, and mechanisms for compensating distributed energy producers are driving the adoption of renewable-friendly grid solutions. International collaboration and standardization of grid technologies are also key to ensuring seamless integration across borders.

Integrating renewables into the grid requires a multifaceted approach that combines technological innovation, infrastructure investment, and policy support. As the share of renewable energy in the global power mix continues to grow, these efforts are critical to ensuring a reliable, efficient, and sustainable energy future.

Energy Storage and Efficiency

Energy storage and efficiency innovations are revolutionizing how energy is utilized and managed, ensuring a more reliable and sustainable energy future.

Battery Storage Technologies

Battery storage technologies are a cornerstone of modern energy systems, enabling the effective utilization of renewable energy by storing excess power and delivering it when needed. As renewable energy sources like solar and wind become more prevalent, the ability to store energy efficiently and cost-effectively has become critical for maintaining grid stability and meeting energy demand during periods of low generation. Innovations in battery technology are addressing these challenges, transforming the way energy is stored and managed.

Lithium-ion batteries are currently the most widely used technology for energy storage, thanks to their high energy density, long cycle life, and declining costs. These batteries have been extensively deployed in residential, commercial, and grid-scale applications. Lithium-ion batteries are particularly effective in pairing with solar panels and wind turbines, storing excess energy generated during peak production hours for use during periods of low generation. Advances in manufacturing processes and material science are continually improving their performance, safety, and affordability.

Flow batteries are another emerging technology gaining attention for large-scale energy storage. Unlike lithium-ion batteries, which store energy in solid electrodes, flow batteries use liquid electrolytes stored in external tanks. This design allows for scalability by increasing the size of the tanks, making flow batteries ideal for long-duration storage applications. Additionally, flow batteries have a long operational life and can endure deep discharges without significant degradation, making them suitable for grid-level energy management.

Solid-state batteries represent a breakthrough in battery technology, offering higher energy density, faster charging times, and improved safety compared to conventional lithium-ion batteries. These batteries replace the liquid electrolyte found in traditional designs with a solid electrolyte, eliminating risks such as leakage and thermal runaway. Solid-state batteries are being actively developed for applications ranging from consumer electronics to electric vehicles and grid storage.

Beyond these mainstream technologies, research is advancing into alternative battery chemistries, such as sodium-ion, zinc-air, and lithium-sulfur batteries. Sodium-ion batteries, for instance, are gaining attention as a more sustainable and cost-effective alternative to lithium-ion, given the abundance and low cost of sodium. Zinc-air batteries, which use oxygen from the air as a reactant, offer high energy density and are being explored for applications requiring long-duration energy storage.

Battery storage technologies are also being integrated with digital tools to enhance their functionality. Smart energy management systems enable real-time monitoring and optimization of battery performance, ensuring efficient energy use and extended battery life. AI and machine learning algorithms are increasingly being employed to predict energy demand and automate energy dispatch, maximizing the benefits of storage systems.

The deployment of battery storage technologies is further supported by policy incentives and market mechanisms. Government subsidies, tax credits, and renewable energy mandates are accelerating the adoption of storage systems, while energy markets are evolving to reward the flexibility and reliability provided by advanced storage solutions.

As battery storage technologies continue to evolve, they are becoming indispensable in the global transition to renewable energy, addressing challenges of intermittency and enhancing the resilience of energy systems. These innovations are paving the way for a sustainable energy future.

Energy Efficiency Solutions in Buildings and Industries

Energy efficiency solutions are pivotal for reducing energy consumption and lowering greenhouse gas emissions in buildings and industries. As global energy demand continues to rise, these solutions help optimize resource use, cut operational costs, and contribute to sustainability goals across sectors. Advances in technology, design, and management practices are driving significant improvements in energy efficiency.

In buildings, energy efficiency begins with the design and construction process. Passive design strategies, such as optimizing building orientation, using natural lighting, and enhancing insulation, reduce the need for artificial heating, cooling, and lighting. High-performance materials, such as double-glazed windows and reflective roofing, minimize heat transfer and improve thermal comfort. Advanced building envelope technologies, including airtight construction and energy-efficient facades, further enhance efficiency by reducing energy loss.

Heating, ventilation, and air conditioning (HVAC) systems are among the largest energy consumers in buildings. Modern energy-efficient HVAC systems incorporate variable-speed motors, smart thermostats, and heat recovery systems to optimize performance while minimizing energy use. Additionally, integrating renewable energy sources, such as solar panels for water heating or powering HVAC systems, further reduces reliance on conventional energy sources.

Lighting systems have also seen significant advancements. LED lighting technology, which consumes significantly less energy than traditional incandescent or fluorescent bulbs, is becoming standard in residential, commercial, and industrial buildings. Smart lighting systems equipped with motion sensors and daylight harvesting features adjust lighting levels automatically, ensuring energy is used only when and where it is needed.

Energy management systems (EMS) are revolutionizing energy efficiency in buildings and industries. These digital platforms monitor, analyze, and optimize energy use in real-time, providing actionable insights to reduce waste. EMS can integrate with smart grids to respond to demand fluctuations, shifting energy use to off-peak hours or prioritizing renewable energy sources.

In industrial settings, energy efficiency solutions focus on optimizing processes and equipment. High-efficiency motors, compressors, and pumps reduce energy consumption in manufacturing and other industrial operations. Waste heat recovery systems capture and reuse heat generated during industrial processes, converting it into usable energy for heating, cooling, or electricity generation. Similarly, cogeneration systems, or combined heat and power (CHP), simultaneously produce electricity and useful heat, achieving higher overall efficiency than conventional power generation.

Process optimization technologies, such as advanced sensors, automation, and AI, are enabling industries to monitor and fine-tune operations for maximum energy efficiency. Predictive maintenance systems use AI to identify potential equipment failures before they occur, ensuring machinery operates at peak efficiency and avoiding energy-intensive breakdowns.

Regulatory standards and certification programs further support energy efficiency efforts. Building codes mandate minimum energy performance requirements, while certifications like LEED (Leadership in Energy and Environmental Design) and ISO 50001 provide frameworks for achieving and verifying energy efficiency improvements.

Through a combination of innovative technologies, smart management practices, and supportive policies, energy efficiency solutions in buildings and industries are playing a critical role in reducing energy demand and promoting sustainability. These solutions are not only reducing costs but also accelerating the global transition to low-carbon energy systems.

Future Trends in Energy Storage

Energy storage technologies are evolving rapidly to meet the growing demands of renewable energy integration, grid reliability, and energy independence. Future trends in energy storage focus on enhancing efficiency, scalability, affordability, and sustainability, driven by innovations in materials, designs, and applications. These advancements are poised to transform how energy is stored and utilized across sectors.

One significant trend is the continued evolution of lithium-ion batteries. While they dominate the current market, future developments aim to address challenges such as resource scarcity and environmental impact. Innovations in anode and cathode materials, such as silicon or lithium metal anodes, are expected to increase energy density and extend battery life. Recycling technologies are also being advanced to recover valuable materials from used batteries, reducing reliance on mining and enhancing the sustainability of lithium-ion systems.

Beyond lithium-ion, alternative battery chemistries are emerging as promising solutions for specific applications. Sodium-ion batteries, for example, use abundant and inexpensive materials, making them a cost-effective option for stationary energy storage. Solid-state batteries, which replace liquid electrolytes with solid materials, offer improved safety, higher energy density, and faster charging times.

These features make solid-state batteries particularly attractive for EVs and grid-scale storage.

Flow batteries are another area of innovation. These systems, which use liquid electrolytes stored in external tanks, provide scalable energy storage for long-duration applications. Future developments in flow batteries focus on increasing energy density, reducing costs, and improving efficiency. Organic flow batteries, which use renewable and biodegradable materials, are being explored to enhance environmental sustainability.

Hydrogen energy storage is gaining attention as a versatile and long-term solution. Surplus renewable energy can be used to produce green hydrogen through electrolysis, which is then stored and later converted back to electricity or used as a fuel. Advances in electrolyzer efficiency and hydrogen storage materials, such as metal-organic frameworks, are expected to accelerate the adoption of hydrogen as a viable energy storage option.

Energy storage systems are also becoming more integrated with digital technologies. AI and machine learning are being utilized to optimize energy storage operations, predict demand, and enhance battery performance. These tools enable real-time monitoring and dynamic energy management, improving the efficiency and reliability of storage systems. Blockchain technology is also being applied to facilitate peer-to-peer energy trading and ensure transparency in energy transactions.

Sustainability is a key focus for future energy storage systems. Researchers are developing batteries with reduced environmental footprints by using non-toxic, recyclable, or renewable materials. Efforts to design modular and reusable storage systems aim to minimize waste and extend the lifecycle of energy storage technologies.

As renewable energy penetration continues to grow, the demand for advanced and sustainable energy storage solutions will intensify.

The future of energy storage lies in a combination of technological breakthroughs, digital integration, and sustainable practices, ensuring that energy storage systems can meet the evolving needs of a decarbonized and resilient energy future.

Policy and Investment in Renewable Energy

Policy and investment in renewable energy are essential drivers of the global transition to sustainable energy systems, shaping the development and adoption of innovative technologies.

Role of Policy in Driving Renewable Adoption

Policy plays a pivotal role in accelerating the adoption of renewable energy by creating a regulatory framework and incentives that promote clean energy technologies. Governments and international organizations design and implement policies to address barriers, encourage investment, and establish long-term goals for renewable energy development. These measures are critical for transforming energy markets and transitioning to sustainable energy systems.

Renewable energy mandates, such as Renewable Portfolio Standards (RPS), require utilities to source a specific percentage of their electricity from renewable sources. These mandates create a guaranteed market for renewable energy, incentivizing utilities to invest in solar, wind, and other clean technologies. Similarly, feed-in tariffs (FiTs) guarantee fixed payments for renewable energy producers, ensuring financial viability for renewable projects and encouraging participation from diverse stakeholders.

Subsidies and tax incentives are widely used to reduce the cost of renewable energy projects. Investment tax credits (ITCs) and production tax credits (PTCs) lower the upfront and operational costs of renewable installations, making them more competitive with fossil fuels. Grants and low-interest loans provide additional financial support, particularly for community-scale and innovative projects.

Regulatory policies also include carbon pricing mechanisms, such as carbon taxes or cap-and-trade systems, which penalize greenhouse gas emissions and make renewable energy more economically attractive. By internalizing the environmental costs of fossil fuels, these policies level the playing field for renewables and drive market shifts toward cleaner energy sources.

In addition, national and international renewable energy targets provide clear direction for industry and investors, fostering confidence in the long-term growth of renewable markets. These targets are often integrated into broader climate policies, reinforcing commitments to reducing carbon emissions and addressing global environmental challenges.

Investment Strategies for Green Energy

Investment strategies for green energy are designed to mobilize capital toward renewable energy projects, ensuring their development, scalability, and long-term viability. These strategies focus on attracting private sector funding, leveraging public resources, and fostering innovation to accelerate the global transition to clean energy.

Public-private partnerships (PPPs) are a cornerstone of green energy investment strategies. Governments provide initial funding or guarantees to reduce financial risks for private investors, encouraging their participation in renewable energy projects. These partnerships facilitate the deployment of large-scale projects, such as offshore wind farms or solar energy parks, by combining public resources with private sector expertise and capital.

Green bonds are another effective investment strategy. These fixed-income financial instruments are issued to raise funds specifically for environmental and renewable energy projects. Green bonds attract environmentally conscious investors and provide a transparent framework for financing renewable initiatives, ensuring accountability and measurable impacts.

Institutional investors, including pension funds and insurance companies, are increasingly allocating capital to renewable energy assets. These investments are driven by the stable returns and long-term growth potential of green energy projects. To support this trend, governments and financial institutions are developing new investment vehicles, such as renewable energy investment trusts and green infrastructure funds, to make it easier for institutional and retail investors to participate.

Additionally, venture capital and private equity firms play a critical role in supporting early-stage green energy innovations. By providing funding to startups and emerging technologies, these investors drive the development and commercialization of next-generation renewable energy solutions, ensuring continued progress in the sector.

Chapter 3: Artificial Intelligence in Sustainability

AI is transforming the sustainability landscape by offering innovative solutions to complex environmental challenges. From optimizing energy use and enhancing resource management to monitoring biodiversity and predicting climate patterns, AI is enabling more efficient and informed decision-making across industries. This chapter explores the diverse applications of AI in advancing sustainability, including its role in agriculture, green manufacturing, and environmental conservation. It also addresses the ethical considerations and challenges associated with AI deployment, providing a comprehensive overview of how this powerful technology is driving progress toward a sustainable future.

AI for Environmental Monitoring

AI for environmental monitoring leverages advanced technologies to track, analyze, and address environmental changes with unprecedented precision and efficiency.

Applications in Climate Modeling

AI is revolutionizing climate modeling by enhancing the accuracy, speed, and scalability of predictions about climate systems and their interactions. Traditional climate models rely on complex mathematical equations and computationally intensive simulations to predict future climate scenarios. While effective, these models often require significant time and resources to produce results. AI introduces a new dimension to climate modeling by using machine learning algorithms to process large datasets and identify patterns that can improve the precision and efficiency of climate predictions.

One of the primary applications of AI in climate modeling is in forecasting weather and extreme events. Machine learning algorithms analyze historical weather data, satellite imagery, and real-time observations to predict short-term and long-term weather patterns with high accuracy. These predictions are particularly useful for preparing for extreme events such as hurricanes, floods, and heatwaves, enabling better disaster response and risk management.

AI also enhances Earth system models by integrating diverse datasets, such as ocean currents, atmospheric conditions, and land-use changes, into a cohesive framework. Neural networks and deep learning techniques can uncover nonlinear relationships between variables, improving the understanding of how different components of the climate system interact. This leads to more accurate projections of phenomena like sea-level rise, glacier melt, and ecosystem changes.

Another significant application is the development of high-resolution climate models. Traditional models often operate at coarse spatial resolutions due to computational limitations, which can obscure localized climate impacts. AI-powered downscaling techniques use machine learning to refine these models, generating high-resolution projections that capture regional and local climate variations. This is particularly valuable for assessing climate impacts on specific communities, ecosystems, or infrastructure projects.

AI is also being used to improve carbon cycle modeling, which is essential for understanding the dynamics of greenhouse gas emissions and their impact on climate systems. Machine learning algorithms analyze large datasets of carbon flux measurements, satellite observations, and land-use data to predict how carbon emissions and sequestration will evolve under different scenarios. This helps policymakers design effective strategies for reducing emissions and enhancing carbon sinks.

In addition, AI facilitates real-time monitoring of climate changes by processing data from satellites, drones, and IoT sensors. These tools provide continuous updates on parameters such as temperature, humidity, and atmospheric composition, feeding data into climate models for dynamic adjustments. This capability is particularly important for tracking rapidly evolving phenomena like Arctic ice melt or deforestation rates.

Despite these advancements, integrating AI into climate modeling also poses challenges, such as the need for extensive training data and the risk of algorithmic biases. However, ongoing research and development aim to address these issues, ensuring that AI continues to enhance the predictive power and reliability of climate models.

By complementing traditional methods with advanced machine learning techniques, AI is transforming climate modeling into a faster, more precise, and highly scalable tool for understanding and addressing global climate challenges. This integration is providing critical insights to guide mitigation and adaptation strategies in the face of climate change.

AI for Biodiversity Conservation

AI is playing a transformative role in biodiversity conservation, offering powerful tools to monitor, analyze, and protect ecosystems and species. By leveraging vast amounts of data and advanced computational capabilities, AI enables conservationists to address biodiversity challenges with greater precision and efficiency than ever before.

One of the key applications of AI in biodiversity conservation is wildlife monitoring. AI-powered cameras and sensors equipped with machine learning algorithms can automatically identify and track species in their natural habitats. These systems analyze images, videos, and audio recordings to detect animal presence, behavior, and population trends. For example, acoustic monitoring tools use AI to identify species-specific calls, providing critical information about elusive or nocturnal species that are difficult to observe directly.

Satellite imagery and remote sensing technologies, combined with AI, are being used to map and monitor ecosystems on a global scale.

Machine learning algorithms process high-resolution images to detect changes in land use, deforestation, and habitat fragmentation. These tools provide real-time insights into how human activities are impacting biodiversity and help prioritize conservation efforts in the most threatened areas. AI also facilitates the mapping of critical habitats and migration corridors, ensuring that conservation plans align with species' ecological needs.

Predictive analytics powered by AI are being used to model biodiversity trends and anticipate future risks. By analyzing historical data on species populations, climate conditions, and habitat changes, AI can predict how species and ecosystems will respond to various environmental stressors. These predictions help inform proactive conservation strategies, such as habitat restoration, protected area designation, and species reintroduction programs.

AI is also revolutionizing the fight against illegal wildlife trade and poaching. Algorithms analyze patterns in illegal trade networks and track suspicious activities on online platforms, enabling law enforcement agencies to identify and intercept traffickers. Additionally, AI-powered drones and camera traps equipped with facial recognition software are being deployed to monitor protected areas and detect poaching activities in real time. These technologies enhance the ability of conservationists and rangers to safeguard vulnerable species from human threats.

Invasive species management is another area where AI is making a significant impact. Machine learning models can predict the spread of invasive species and assess their ecological impacts, enabling early detection and intervention. AI tools also help prioritize management actions, ensuring resources are allocated effectively to mitigate the threats posed by invasive organisms.

Citizen science initiatives are benefiting from AI integration, as platforms equipped with machine learning enable non-experts to contribute to biodiversity data collection. Apps and online tools use AI to identify species from photos or audio recordings submitted by the public, expanding the reach and scale of biodiversity monitoring efforts.

While AI offers immense potential for biodiversity conservation, challenges such as data availability, algorithm biases, and ethical considerations must be addressed. Despite these hurdles, AI continues to enhance the ability of conservationists to understand and protect the natural world, making it an indispensable tool in the fight to preserve global biodiversity.

AI in Green Manufacturing

AI in green manufacturing is transforming production processes by optimizing resource use, reducing waste, and enhancing energy efficiency.

Reducing Waste Through AI Optimization

AI is revolutionizing waste reduction in manufacturing by streamlining processes, improving efficiency, and minimizing resource use. By leveraging data-driven insights and advanced algorithms, AI enables manufacturers to identify inefficiencies, predict potential waste, and implement targeted strategies to reduce it across the production cycle.

One significant application of AI in waste reduction is in predictive analytics. AI systems analyze historical and real-time production data to forecast potential bottlenecks, defects, or material wastage before they occur. For instance, predictive maintenance powered by AI identifies machinery issues that could lead to defective products or downtime, allowing manufacturers to address problems proactively. This not only prevents waste but also extends the lifespan of equipment.

AI-powered quality control systems are another critical tool in minimizing waste. These systems use computer vision and machine learning to inspect products at various stages of production, identifying defects with greater accuracy and speed than human inspectors. Early detection of flaws prevents defective items from progressing through the production line, reducing material waste and associated costs.

Inventory management is also optimized through AI, which analyzes demand patterns, production schedules, and supply chain data to ensure the right materials are available at the right time. This minimizes overstocking or underutilization of raw materials, reducing waste and improving resource efficiency. AI systems can also recommend alternative materials or processes that achieve the same output with fewer resources.

In addition, AI enhances process optimization by analyzing workflows and identifying areas for improvement. Machine learning models can suggest adjustments to production parameters, such as temperature, pressure, or speed, to maximize resource use and minimize waste. For example, AI in additive manufacturing (3D printing) optimizes material usage by generating precise designs and identifying the most efficient ways to produce components, reducing excess material.

Energy efficiency is another area where AI contributes to waste reduction. AI systems monitor energy consumption throughout the production process, identifying areas of inefficiency and suggesting adjustments. By optimizing energy use, manufacturers not only reduce their carbon footprint but also avoid the waste associated with unnecessary energy consumption.

AI also supports circular manufacturing practices by identifying opportunities to reuse or recycle materials within the production process. Algorithms can classify and sort waste materials, enabling manufacturers to reintegrate them into the production cycle or divert them for recycling. This reduces the volume of waste sent to landfills and promotes a closed-loop system that maximizes resource use.

Supply chain optimization is another area where AI reduces waste. By analyzing logistics data, AI systems streamline transportation, storage, and delivery processes, minimizing waste associated with overproduction, excess packaging, and inefficient distribution. Real-time tracking and forecasting further ensure that resources are allocated efficiently across the supply chain.

Through advanced data analysis and automation, AI enables manufacturers to achieve significant reductions in material, energy, and resource waste. These innovations not only improve operational efficiency but also contribute to sustainable practices that align with the growing demand for environmentally responsible manufacturing.

Predictive Maintenance for Sustainability

Predictive maintenance, driven by AI and machine learning, is transforming the way industries approach equipment maintenance, promoting sustainability by reducing energy use, material waste, and operational inefficiencies. Unlike traditional maintenance approaches, which rely on scheduled or reactive repairs, predictive maintenance uses real-time data and advanced analytics to anticipate equipment failures before they occur, allowing for timely interventions.

One of the primary ways predictive maintenance contributes to sustainability is by extending the lifespan of machinery and equipment. Sensors embedded in industrial machines continuously monitor parameters such as temperature, vibration, and pressure. These sensors collect data that AI systems analyze to identify patterns and anomalies indicative of potential failures. By addressing these issues early, manufacturers can prevent wear and tear from escalating, reducing the need for frequent replacements and conserving resources used in manufacturing new parts.

Energy efficiency is another key benefit of predictive maintenance. Machines operating under optimal conditions consume less energy, whereas faulty or poorly maintained equipment tends to draw more power. Predictive maintenance ensures that equipment operates efficiently by identifying and resolving energy-draining issues, such as misaligned components or deteriorating bearings. This not only lowers operational costs but also reduces the carbon footprint of industrial processes.

Material waste is also minimized through predictive maintenance. Unscheduled breakdowns can lead to production disruptions, resulting in unfinished or defective products that are discarded as waste. By proactively addressing equipment issues, predictive maintenance prevents such disruptions, ensuring that raw materials are used efficiently and that product quality is maintained.

Predictive maintenance also reduces downtime, a critical factor in sustainable operations. By scheduling maintenance activities based on actual equipment conditions rather than fixed intervals, businesses can minimize disruptions to production processes. This approach optimizes resource allocation, reduces idle time, and ensures continuous output, thereby improving overall operational efficiency.

The integration of predictive maintenance with digital twins further enhances its effectiveness. Digital twins are virtual replicas of physical systems that use real-time data to simulate and predict performance. When combined with AI-powered predictive maintenance, digital twins enable manufacturers to visualize potential failures and evaluate corrective actions without interrupting operations. This not only improves accuracy but also reduces trial-and-error approaches that waste resources.

Supply chain sustainability also benefits from predictive maintenance. Reliable equipment reduces the risk of delays and disruptions in production schedules, ensuring that supply chains function smoothly. This prevents the waste associated with expedited shipping, overproduction, and stockpiling caused by unexpected equipment failures.

AI-driven predictive maintenance supports a circular economy by enabling the reuse and refurbishment of components. When maintenance needs are accurately predicted, manufacturers can repair and repurpose parts instead of discarding them, reducing waste and conserving valuable resources.

By fostering efficient and reliable operations, predictive maintenance aligns industrial practices with sustainability goals. Through its ability to optimize energy use, minimize waste, and enhance equipment performance, predictive maintenance is a vital tool in achieving greener, more sustainable industrial processes.

AI for Sustainable Agriculture

AI for sustainable agriculture is revolutionizing farming practices by enhancing efficiency, optimizing resource use, and supporting environmentally friendly food production.

Precision Farming Techniques

Precision farming techniques, driven by advanced technologies and data analytics, are transforming agriculture by optimizing resource use, improving crop yields, and minimizing environmental impact. These techniques leverage real-time data, satellite imagery, sensors, and AI to enable farmers to make informed decisions tailored to specific conditions in their fields.

One of the core components of precision farming is the use of remote sensing technologies. Satellites and drones equipped with multispectral cameras capture detailed images of farmland, providing insights into soil health, crop conditions, and moisture levels. AI algorithms analyze these images to identify patterns and anomalies, such as nutrient deficiencies or pest infestations, allowing farmers to address issues proactively. By targeting specific areas, farmers can apply fertilizers, pesticides, and water more efficiently, reducing waste and environmental harm.

Soil sensors are another critical tool in precision farming. These sensors monitor key parameters such as pH levels, moisture content, and nutrient availability in real time. The data collected helps farmers determine the precise amount of water and fertilizers needed for optimal plant growth. Variable rate technology (VRT) integrates this information into farm equipment, enabling the targeted application of inputs with pinpoint accuracy. This reduces overuse, lowers costs, and prevents runoff that can harm surrounding ecosystems.

GPS technology plays a vital role in precision farming by enabling automated guidance systems for tractors and other machinery. These systems ensure accurate planting, harvesting, and input application, reducing overlaps and gaps in field operations. Precision planting, for instance, optimizes seed spacing and depth based on soil conditions, ensuring uniform crop emergence and maximizing yield potential.

Weather data integration is another aspect of precision farming that supports sustainable practices. AI-driven platforms analyze historical and real-time weather data to provide accurate forecasts and recommendations for planting, irrigation, and harvesting schedules. This minimizes risks associated with adverse weather events and ensures that farming operations are aligned with optimal environmental conditions.

Livestock management has also benefited from precision farming techniques. Wearable sensors and monitoring systems track the health, behavior, and productivity of livestock, enabling farmers to identify and address issues such as disease outbreaks or nutritional deficiencies promptly. Precision feeding systems use AI to tailor feed rations to the specific needs of individual animals, improving efficiency and reducing waste.

Machine learning algorithms are increasingly used to predict crop performance and optimize farming practices. These models analyze historical data on yields, soil conditions, and weather patterns to recommend strategies for enhancing productivity. Predictive analytics also helps farmers select the best crop varieties for their specific conditions, reducing the risk of crop failure and improving resilience to climate change.

Precision farming techniques not only improve agricultural efficiency but also promote environmental sustainability. By reducing resource waste and minimizing the ecological footprint of farming operations, these techniques ensure that agricultural practices are more sustainable and resilient to future challenges. Through the integration of technology and data-driven decision-making, precision farming is revolutionizing the way food is produced and contributing to a more sustainable agricultural future.

AI-Driven Resource Management

AI-driven resource management is transforming agriculture by optimizing the use of critical inputs such as water, fertilizers, and energy, ensuring sustainable and efficient farming practices. By leveraging advanced algorithms, real-time data, and predictive analytics, AI enables farmers to allocate resources more precisely, reducing waste and enhancing productivity.

One of the primary applications of AI in resource management is precision irrigation. AI systems analyze data from weather forecasts, soil moisture sensors, and crop growth patterns to determine the exact amount of water needed for optimal plant health. These systems provide recommendations or automate irrigation schedules, ensuring that water is applied only where and when it is required. This approach minimizes water waste, reduces energy consumption from irrigation pumps, and prevents waterlogging or nutrient runoff, which can harm surrounding ecosystems.

Fertilizer management is another area where AI is making a significant impact. Machine learning models process data from soil sensors, satellite imagery, and historical yield patterns to identify nutrient deficiencies and recommend targeted fertilizer applications.

43

VRT integrates AI-driven recommendations into farm machinery, enabling site-specific fertilizer distribution. This reduces the overuse of fertilizers, lowers costs, and prevents environmental issues such as soil degradation and water pollution caused by nutrient runoff.

AI also enhances pest and disease management by analyzing data from sensors, drones, and cameras to detect early signs of infestations or crop diseases. Predictive models assess the likelihood of outbreaks based on weather conditions, crop growth stages, and historical patterns. Farmers receive alerts and tailored action plans, allowing them to deploy pesticides or biological controls only in affected areas. This targeted approach minimizes chemical use, reduces environmental impact, and preserves beneficial organisms in the ecosystem.

Energy management in agriculture has also been improved through AI-driven solutions. Smart energy systems analyze data on energy consumption patterns, weather forecasts, and operational schedules to optimize energy use in farming operations. For example, AI can determine the best times to run irrigation pumps, greenhouse climate control systems, or machinery based on energy demand and availability. By aligning energy use with renewable energy production or off-peak grid hours, these systems reduce costs and the carbon footprint of agricultural practices.

AI-driven resource management also supports sustainable land use planning. By integrating data on soil quality, topography, and climate conditions, AI models identify the most suitable crops or practices for specific plots of land. This ensures that resources are used efficiently while minimizing soil degradation and maximizing yields.

Furthermore, AI-powered platforms enable real-time monitoring and decision-making, providing farmers with actionable insights via mobile apps or dashboards. These tools empower farmers to make informed decisions quickly, adapting resource use to changing conditions and improving overall farm efficiency.

Through the precise allocation of water, nutrients, energy, and other inputs, AI-driven resource management is reshaping agriculture into a more sustainable and resilient industry. By reducing waste and enhancing productivity, these technologies help address the growing demand for food while preserving critical natural resources for future generations.

Addressing Food Security Challenges

AI is playing a transformative role in addressing food security challenges by enhancing agricultural productivity, reducing food waste, and improving the resilience of food systems. As the global population continues to grow and climate change intensifies, ensuring a stable and sufficient food supply has become a critical priority. AI technologies offer innovative solutions to meet these challenges by optimizing resource use, increasing efficiency, and reducing losses across the food supply chain.

One key application of AI in addressing food security is precision agriculture, which enables farmers to maximize crop yields while minimizing resource inputs. AI systems analyze data from sensors, drones, and satellite imagery to monitor soil health, crop conditions, and weather patterns in real time. These insights allow farmers to make data-driven decisions about planting, irrigation, fertilization, and pest control, ensuring that resources are used efficiently and crops are grown under optimal conditions. By improving productivity on existing farmland, AI helps reduce the pressure to convert natural ecosystems into agricultural land.

AI also contributes to addressing food security by tackling post-harvest losses and food waste. Machine learning algorithms can analyze data on supply chain logistics, market demand, and storage conditions to optimize the transportation and storage of perishable goods. For example, AI-powered monitoring systems track temperature, humidity, and other environmental factors in storage facilities to ensure that food remains fresh during transit. Predictive models identify potential spoilage risks and recommend interventions to prevent losses, reducing waste and ensuring that more food reaches consumers.

In addition, AI enhances the efficiency and sustainability of food distribution networks. Algorithms optimize supply chain routes, reducing transportation costs and greenhouse gas emissions while ensuring timely delivery of food to markets. AI-driven demand forecasting tools analyze consumption patterns, market trends, and weather data to predict food demand accurately. This helps producers and retailers align production and distribution with consumer needs, minimizing overproduction and food surplus that often leads to waste.

AI technologies also play a role in improving access to food in vulnerable regions. Predictive models assess the risk of food shortages by analyzing data on crop yields, rainfall, and socio-economic factors. These insights enable governments and humanitarian organizations to identify at-risk populations and implement targeted interventions, such as distributing food aid or investing in local agricultural development. AI-driven platforms also facilitate the equitable distribution of food resources by ensuring transparency and accountability in food aid programs.

AI supports the development of climate-resilient agricultural practices, which are essential for ensuring food security in the face of changing environmental conditions. Machine learning models simulate the impact of climate variables on crop performance, helping farmers select resilient crop varieties and adopt adaptive strategies. Additionally, AI-powered tools aid in the restoration of degraded lands, improving soil health and productivity over time.

By addressing inefficiencies in production, distribution, and consumption, AI is helping to overcome critical food security challenges. These technologies are empowering farmers, businesses, and policymakers to build a more sustainable and resilient global food system, ensuring that food is available, accessible, and affordable for all.

Challenges and Ethical Considerations

The integration of AI in sustainability efforts presents significant challenges and ethical considerations, ranging from data privacy to environmental impacts.

Energy Use and Carbon Footprint of AI

The rapid growth of AI technologies has brought significant advancements across industries, but it also raises concerns about their energy use and carbon footprint. AI systems, particularly those involving machine learning and deep learning, require substantial computational power, which consumes large amounts of energy and contributes to greenhouse gas emissions.

Training AI models is one of the most energy-intensive processes. Complex algorithms, such as deep learning models, demand high-performance hardware like graphics processing units (GPUs) and tensor processing units (TPUs). These systems run continuously for extended periods, consuming electricity that often comes from non-renewable sources. For example, training a single large language model can require energy equivalent to that used by several households in a year. The carbon emissions associated with this process are significant, particularly in regions where fossil fuels dominate the energy mix.

The operational use of AI systems also contributes to their carbon footprint. AI applications that process real-time data, run predictive models, or analyze massive datasets rely on data centers with extensive infrastructure. These data centers are energy-intensive, requiring electricity not only to power servers but also to cool equipment to prevent overheating. While some companies have adopted renewable energy and energy-efficient practices, many data centers still rely on traditional energy sources, amplifying the environmental impact of AI operations.

The growing demand for AI technologies highlights the importance of addressing their energy consumption and carbon footprint. As AI adoption expands, sustainable practices in model training, hardware development, and data center operations are critical for minimizing their environmental impact.

Bias and Fairness in AI Applications

Bias and fairness in AI applications have become critical concerns as AI systems increasingly influence decision-making in various sectors, including sustainability. Bias occurs when AI algorithms produce outcomes that unfairly favor or disadvantage certain groups, often due to imbalances or inaccuracies in the data used to train these models. This issue not only undermines the credibility of AI systems but also raises ethical and social challenges.

One major source of bias in AI is the use of datasets that do not represent diverse populations or environments. For example, if an AI model designed for environmental monitoring is trained on data collected only from specific regions, it may produce inaccurate results when applied to other areas with different ecological conditions. Such biases can lead to ineffective or harmful policy decisions, disproportionately impacting vulnerable communities.

Algorithmic bias can also arise from the methods used to process and analyze data. Certain features or patterns in the data may be emphasized over others, reflecting the priorities or assumptions of the developers rather than objective criteria. This can result in unfair outcomes, such as misallocating resources in sustainability projects or overlooking the needs of marginalized groups.

Ensuring fairness in AI applications requires deliberate efforts to identify and mitigate biases at every stage of development. Strategies include diversifying training datasets, implementing fairness metrics during model evaluation, and involving multidisciplinary teams to oversee AI deployment. Transparent and accountable practices are essential for addressing these biases and building trust in AI systems.

Chapter 4: Blockchain for Sustainability

Blockchain technology is emerging as a powerful tool for advancing sustainability by enhancing transparency, accountability, and efficiency across industries. Its decentralized and secure nature enables innovative applications in supply chain management, renewable energy trading, and resource conservation. This chapter explores how blockchain is being utilized to address key environmental challenges, its role in fostering sustainable practices, and the potential limitations and ethical considerations associated with its implementation. Through these discussions, the chapter highlights blockchain's transformative potential in building a more sustainable and equitable future.

Blockchain Basics and Sustainability

Blockchain technology, with its decentralized and transparent structure, offers innovative solutions to address sustainability challenges across various sectors.

Overview of Blockchain Technology

Blockchain technology is a decentralized digital ledger that securely records transactions across multiple computers, ensuring transparency, immutability, and trust without the need for intermediaries. Originally developed as the underlying technology for cryptocurrencies like Bitcoin, blockchain has evolved to support a wide range of applications across industries, including finance, supply chain management, and sustainability.

At its core, blockchain operates as a series of interconnected blocks, each containing a list of transactions. Once a block is filled, it is validated by a network of participants, known as nodes, using consensus mechanisms such as proof-of-work or proof-of-stake. Once validated, the block is added to the chain, creating a permanent and unalterable record. This distributed architecture eliminates the risks associated with centralized systems, such as data tampering or single points of failure.

The transparency of blockchain is a key feature that makes it particularly valuable for sustainability applications. Every transaction recorded on a blockchain is visible to all participants in the network, fostering accountability and trust. Additionally, the technology's security ensures that data cannot be altered or deleted once it has been recorded, making blockchain an ideal solution for tracking and verifying ESG metrics.

Smart contracts, another fundamental component of blockchain, automate processes by executing predefined actions when certain conditions are met. These self-executing contracts enhance efficiency and reduce administrative overhead, further expanding blockchain's potential for driving innovation and sustainability. Blockchain's versatility continues to unlock transformative possibilities across industries worldwide.

Blockchain's Potential in Sustainability

Blockchain technology holds immense potential for advancing sustainability by providing transparency, accountability, and efficiency in managing resources and addressing environmental challenges. Its decentralized and secure nature enables innovative solutions that transform industries and drive progress toward sustainable development goals.

One key application of blockchain in sustainability is enhancing supply chain transparency. By recording every step of a product's journey on an immutable ledger, blockchain enables consumers and businesses to verify the ethical and sustainable sourcing of materials. This technology ensures that information about labor practices, environmental impact, and resource use is accurate and accessible, promoting accountability and fostering trust.

In renewable energy markets, blockchain facilitates peer-to-peer energy trading and certifies the origin of green energy. Homeowners with solar panels, for example, can sell excess energy directly to neighbors through blockchain-based platforms. These systems eliminate intermediaries, reduce transaction costs, and create more efficient energy markets. Blockchain also supports the tracking and trading of renewable energy certificates, ensuring compliance with sustainability targets.

Blockchain's role in resource conservation extends to areas such as water management and waste reduction. By monitoring usage and recording data in real time, blockchain can help optimize resource allocation, reduce waste, and incentivize sustainable behaviors.

Additionally, blockchain enhances carbon offset programs by creating verifiable and transparent records of emissions reductions. This prevents double-counting and fraud, ensuring the integrity of carbon markets and encouraging broader participation in climate mitigation efforts. Blockchain's versatility and security make it a powerful tool for fostering sustainability in diverse contexts.

Blockchain in Supply Chain Transparency

Blockchain technology is revolutionizing supply chain transparency by enabling secure, traceable, and tamper-proof records of every step in the production and distribution process.

Tracking Sustainable Sourcing

Blockchain technology is transforming the way sustainable sourcing is tracked and verified, offering unprecedented transparency and accountability across supply chains. By recording every stage of a product's journey on an immutable and decentralized ledger, blockchain ensures that information about sourcing practices, labor conditions, and environmental impact is accurate, accessible, and tamper-proof. This capability is particularly valuable for industries such as agriculture, fashion, and electronics, where sustainability concerns are critical.

One of the key benefits of blockchain in tracking sustainable sourcing is its ability to provide end-to-end visibility in supply chains. Each transaction, from the harvesting of raw materials to the delivery of the final product, is recorded on the blockchain. For example, in the coffee industry, blockchain can document the origin of coffee beans, the conditions under which they were grown, and the journey they took to reach consumers. This information is crucial for ensuring that sourcing practices align with sustainability standards, such as fair trade or organic certification.

Smart contracts, a core feature of blockchain, further enhance the tracking of sustainable sourcing. These self-executing agreements automatically enforce compliance with predefined criteria. For instance, a smart contract can verify that raw materials meet specific sustainability benchmarks before approving payment to suppliers. This reduces the need for manual oversight and ensures that sustainability commitments are upheld throughout the supply chain.

Blockchain also facilitates the authentication of sustainability claims, reducing the risk of greenwashing. Companies can use blockchain to provide verifiable proof of their environmental and social initiatives, such as reduced carbon emissions or ethical labor practices. Consumers can scan a QR code on a product to access detailed information about its sourcing and production, empowering them to make informed purchasing decisions.

The integration of IoT devices with blockchain enhances real-time tracking of sustainable sourcing. IoT sensors monitor parameters such as temperature, humidity, and location, ensuring that raw materials and products are handled in environmentally and socially responsible ways. Data from these sensors is automatically recorded on the blockchain, providing a continuous and reliable stream of information.

Blockchain also enables collaboration among stakeholders in the supply chain. Producers, suppliers, manufacturers, and retailers can access a shared ledger that documents sustainability metrics and tracks progress toward common goals. This collaborative approach fosters trust and accountability, encouraging all participants to adhere to sustainability standards.

Moreover, blockchain supports the auditing and certification process for sustainable sourcing. Auditors can access verified and immutable records on the blockchain, streamlining the evaluation of compliance with environmental and social standards. This reduces the time and cost associated with traditional auditing methods while improving the accuracy and reliability of certifications.

By providing a secure and transparent framework for tracking sustainable sourcing, blockchain technology is empowering companies to meet consumer demand for ethical and environmentally friendly products. It ensures that sustainability claims are credible and actionable, driving accountability and progress across global supply chains.

Reducing Waste in Supply Chains

Blockchain technology is emerging as a powerful tool for reducing waste in supply chains by enhancing transparency, efficiency, and accountability. Through its decentralized and immutable ledger, blockchain enables precise tracking and management of resources, helping to minimize inefficiencies, optimize logistics, and reduce unnecessary waste across industries.

One of the primary ways blockchain reduces waste is by improving inventory management. Traditional supply chains often suffer from overproduction, stockpiling, and misallocation of resources, leading to excess inventory and significant waste. Blockchain provides real-time data on inventory levels, demand forecasts, and production schedules, allowing businesses to align supply with demand more accurately. This reduces the risk of overstocking or underutilizing materials, ensuring that resources are used efficiently.

Blockchain also addresses waste caused by spoilage and damage in perishable goods supply chains, such as food and pharmaceuticals. IoT sensors integrated with blockchain monitor critical parameters like temperature, humidity, and handling conditions during transportation and storage. This data is recorded in real time on the blockchain, allowing stakeholders to identify and address issues immediately. For instance, if a shipment's temperature exceeds acceptable limits, alerts can trigger actions to mitigate damage, reducing the amount of spoiled goods.

In addition to monitoring conditions, blockchain facilitates better coordination among supply chain participants. By providing a single source of truth, blockchain ensures that all parties—producers, distributors, retailers, and logistics providers—have access to the same accurate and up-to-date information. This eliminates communication gaps and reduces delays, which often result in wasted resources or missed opportunities to salvage products nearing expiration.

Another significant application of blockchain in waste reduction is the tracking and optimization of reverse logistics. Blockchain systems enable the efficient handling of returns, repairs, and recycling processes by maintaining detailed records of product history and condition. For example, in the electronics industry, blockchain can track the components of returned devices, ensuring that reusable parts are identified and reintegrated into the production cycle. This supports circular economy practices by minimizing the disposal of valuable materials.

Blockchain also reduces administrative waste by automating and streamlining processes through smart contracts. These self-executing agreements enforce predefined conditions, such as payment upon delivery of goods or verification of quality standards. By reducing the need for manual intervention and paperwork, smart contracts save time and resources while preventing errors that could lead to waste.

Fraud and counterfeiting are additional sources of waste in supply chains, as they often result in the disposal of counterfeit products and loss of consumer trust. Blockchain's tamper-proof ledger ensures the authenticity and traceability of goods, preventing fraud and ensuring that only genuine products reach the market. This not only protects consumers but also reduces the financial and material waste associated with counterfeit goods.

By enabling more efficient, transparent, and accountable supply chains, blockchain technology is helping industries address waste at every stage of the supply chain. Its ability to optimize resource use, improve logistics, and support sustainable practices makes it an essential tool for reducing waste and promoting long-term sustainability.

Ensuring Ethical Labor Practices

Blockchain technology is revolutionizing the enforcement and transparency of ethical labor practices across global supply chains. By providing an immutable and decentralized record of transactions and processes, blockchain ensures accountability and traceability at every stage of production, helping to uphold fair labor standards and prevent exploitation.

One key application of blockchain in promoting ethical labor practices is verifying the origins of goods. Blockchain enables companies to track and document the journey of raw materials and products, from sourcing to final delivery. This transparency ensures that suppliers and subcontractors adhere to labor regulations, such as prohibitions on forced labor or child labor. For example, a blockchain ledger can confirm that a particular batch of cotton was harvested by workers earning fair wages under safe working conditions.

Smart contracts play a critical role in ensuring compliance with labor agreements. These self-executing contracts enforce predetermined conditions automatically, such as timely payment to workers or adherence to safety standards. If a supplier fails to meet these requirements, the contract can withhold payment or trigger corrective actions. This automation reduces the risk of noncompliance and strengthens the enforcement of ethical labor practices.

Blockchain also facilitates third-party audits by providing verified and tamper-proof data on labor practices. Auditors can access detailed records of worker wages, hours, and conditions without relying on potentially biased or incomplete information from suppliers. This enhances the credibility and efficiency of audits, ensuring that companies meet their commitments to ethical labor standards.

Worker empowerment is another important aspect of blockchain's role in ethical labor practices. Blockchain-based platforms can securely record grievances, complaints, or violations reported by workers, protecting their anonymity and reducing the risk of retaliation. These platforms create a direct line of communication between workers and organizations, enabling swift responses to labor violations and fostering a culture of accountability.

Blockchain also combats fraud and misrepresentation in labor certifications. Traditional systems often rely on paper documents that can be falsified or manipulated. Blockchain's immutable ledger ensures the authenticity of certifications, such as fair trade or union compliance, by linking them directly to verified data. This eliminates doubts about the credibility of labor claims and helps consumers make informed purchasing decisions.

In addition to ensuring compliance, blockchain supports capacity building and education for suppliers and workers. By integrating training modules or informational resources into blockchain platforms, companies can help their supply chain partners improve labor practices. These tools provide guidance on labor laws, safety protocols, and workers' rights, ensuring that ethical standards are maintained across the supply chain.

Blockchain technology is not without challenges, such as the need for widespread adoption and technical literacy among supply chain participants. However, its potential to ensure ethical labor practices is transformative, offering a secure, transparent, and efficient way to uphold fair labor standards. By fostering accountability and empowering workers, blockchain is reshaping how industries address labor rights and promote ethical practices globally.

Blockchain in Renewable Energy Trading

Blockchain technology is transforming renewable energy trading by enabling transparent, efficient, and decentralized energy markets.

Peer-to-Peer Energy Trading Platforms

Peer-to-peer (P2P) energy trading platforms, powered by blockchain technology, are revolutionizing the way energy is bought, sold, and distributed. These platforms enable individuals and businesses to trade surplus renewable energy directly with one another, bypassing traditional intermediaries like utility companies. By creating decentralized energy markets, P2P platforms promote greater efficiency, lower costs, and broader access to clean energy.

The core of P2P energy trading lies in blockchain's decentralized and immutable ledger. Every transaction, from energy generation to its sale and consumption, is recorded transparently and securely. This eliminates the need for a centralized authority to manage or verify transactions, reducing administrative costs and streamlining the trading process. Blockchain ensures that all participants have equal access to transaction data, fostering trust and accountability in the system.

Smart contracts, a key feature of blockchain, automate energy trading processes on P2P platforms. These self-executing agreements enable seamless transactions by enforcing predefined conditions. For instance, a smart contract might automatically transfer payment to a solar panel owner once a certain amount of energy is delivered to a buyer. This eliminates delays and the need for manual intervention, making transactions more efficient and reliable.

P2P energy trading platforms also integrate IoT devices, such as smart meters, to track and measure energy production and consumption in real time. IoT devices transmit this data to the blockchain, ensuring accurate records and facilitating fair pricing. Participants can monitor their energy usage and generation through user-friendly apps, allowing them to make informed decisions about when to buy or sell energy based on market conditions.

One of the major benefits of P2P energy trading platforms is their ability to empower prosumers—individuals or businesses that both produce and consume energy. Prosumers with renewable energy systems, such as solar panels or wind turbines, can sell excess energy to others in their community, creating new revenue streams. This decentralization reduces dependence on traditional power grids and enhances energy resilience, particularly in areas prone to outages or with limited access to centralized energy infrastructure.

P2P energy trading also encourages the adoption of renewable energy by providing financial incentives for generating clean power. Participants who invest in renewable energy technologies can recover their costs more quickly by selling surplus energy directly to buyers. This accelerates the transition to renewable energy and contributes to the reduction of greenhouse gas emissions.

Additionally, P2P platforms facilitate dynamic pricing, allowing energy prices to reflect real-time supply and demand. Buyers can purchase energy at lower rates during periods of high generation, while sellers can benefit from higher prices during peak demand.

This pricing mechanism creates a balanced and efficient energy market that optimizes resource utilization.

Despite their potential, P2P energy trading platforms face challenges such as regulatory barriers, technical complexity, and the need for widespread adoption. However, their ability to decentralize energy markets, empower consumers, and promote renewable energy makes them a transformative innovation in the transition to a sustainable energy future. Through blockchain and IoT integration, these platforms are reshaping how energy is traded and consumed worldwide.

Blockchain for Energy Certificates

Blockchain technology is transforming the issuance, tracking, and trading of energy certificates, such as Renewable Energy Certificates (RECs) and Guarantees of Origin (GOs). These certificates play a crucial role in verifying the production and consumption of renewable energy, providing a transparent and reliable way to support the global transition to sustainable energy systems. By leveraging blockchain's decentralized and immutable ledger, the management of energy certificates becomes more efficient, transparent, and resistant to fraud.

Traditional energy certificate systems often rely on centralized authorities to issue and verify certificates, which can be time-consuming, prone to errors, and susceptible to fraudulent activities. Blockchain eliminates these inefficiencies by automating the entire process. Each energy certificate is represented as a digital token recorded on the blockchain, ensuring that it is unique, tamper-proof, and traceable throughout its lifecycle.

The transparency of blockchain is a key advantage in managing energy certificates. Every transaction, from the issuance of a certificate to its trading and retirement, is recorded on the blockchain and visible to all participants in the network. This transparency ensures that the same certificate cannot be sold to multiple buyers, addressing the issue of double-counting and enhancing trust in the system. Buyers can verify the origin of the energy they purchase and ensure it aligns with their sustainability goals.

Smart contracts play a pivotal role in blockchain-based energy certificate systems. These self-executing agreements automate processes such as certificate issuance, transfer, and validation. For instance, a smart contract can automatically generate a certificate when a renewable energy producer feeds power into the grid, based on real-time data from smart meters. Similarly, when a certificate is sold, the smart contract ensures that ownership is transferred securely and instantly, reducing administrative overhead and transaction delays.

Blockchain also facilitates the trading of energy certificates on decentralized marketplaces. Producers, buyers, and intermediaries can trade certificates directly, eliminating the need for traditional brokers and reducing associated costs. This decentralized approach fosters greater participation in certificate markets, including by smaller renewable energy producers who may have been excluded from traditional systems due to high fees or complexity.

The integration of IoT devices with blockchain further enhances the reliability of energy certificate systems. IoT sensors collect real-time data on energy generation and consumption, automatically feeding this information into the blockchain. This ensures that certificates are issued based on accurate and verifiable data, strengthening the credibility of the system.

Blockchain also enables cross-border trading of energy certificates, which is particularly valuable in regions with interconnected energy markets. By providing a standardized and transparent framework, blockchain facilitates international collaboration and ensures that renewable energy targets are met efficiently and effectively.

While blockchain-based energy certificate systems face challenges such as scalability and regulatory alignment, their potential to enhance transparency, reduce costs, and prevent fraud makes them a transformative innovation. By streamlining the management of energy certificates, blockchain is driving greater accountability and participation in renewable energy markets, accelerating the shift toward a sustainable energy future.

Challenges and Limitations of Blockchain

The adoption of blockchain technology in sustainability efforts faces significant challenges and limitations, ranging from high energy consumption to regulatory hurdles and scalability issues.

Energy Consumption of Blockchain Networks

Blockchain networks, particularly those using proof-of-work (PoW) consensus mechanisms, are associated with high energy consumption, raising concerns about their environmental impact. PoW, which underpins cryptocurrencies like Bitcoin and Ethereum (prior to Ethereum's transition to proof-of-stake), requires participants known as miners to solve complex mathematical problems to validate transactions and add new blocks to the blockchain. This process, while ensuring network security and decentralization, demands substantial computational power and electricity.

The energy-intensive nature of PoW stems from the competition among miners to solve cryptographic puzzles. Only the first miner to find the correct solution is rewarded, prompting miners to deploy powerful hardware, such as application-specific integrated circuits (ASICs), to maximize their chances of success. These devices operate continuously, consuming vast amounts of energy. As the network grows and competition increases, the difficulty of these puzzles escalates, further driving energy consumption.

The environmental implications of blockchain energy use are particularly concerning in regions where electricity is generated predominantly from fossil fuels. In such cases, the carbon emissions associated with blockchain operations contribute to climate change and negate potential sustainability benefits. Studies have shown that Bitcoin mining alone consumes as much electricity annually as some medium-sized countries, highlighting the scale of the issue.

Efforts to mitigate the energy consumption of blockchain networks include the development and adoption of alternative consensus mechanisms, such as proof-of-stake (PoS), proof-of-authority (PoA), and proof-of-space. PoS, for instance, replaces energy-intensive mining with a system where validators are chosen to create new blocks based on the amount of cryptocurrency they hold and are willing to "stake" as collateral. This approach drastically reduces energy requirements while maintaining security and decentralization.

Additionally, blockchain projects are exploring the use of renewable energy to power mining operations. Solar, wind, and hydroelectric power are increasingly being integrated into mining facilities to minimize their carbon footprint. Some blockchain networks are also incentivizing energy efficiency by rewarding miners who utilize clean energy sources or adopt energy-saving practices.

Another approach to addressing blockchain energy consumption is improving hardware efficiency. Manufacturers of mining equipment are continually developing more energy-efficient ASICs and GPUs to reduce electricity use without compromising performance. Innovations in cooling technologies also play a role in minimizing energy waste, as cooling systems are essential to maintaining optimal operating conditions for mining hardware.

Layer-2 solutions and off-chain scaling mechanisms are further reducing energy demands by minimizing the number of transactions that need to be processed directly on the blockchain. These solutions handle transactions off-chain and only record final states on the main blockchain, significantly lowering the computational requirements.

While blockchain energy consumption remains a critical challenge, ongoing research and technological advancements are working toward more sustainable solutions. The transition to less energy-intensive consensus mechanisms, adoption of renewable energy, and development of efficient hardware are all contributing to reducing the environmental impact of blockchain networks. By addressing these challenges, blockchain can become a more viable tool for sustainability and innovation without exacerbating global energy concerns.

Scalability and Regulatory Hurdles

Scalability and regulatory hurdles are two critical challenges that blockchain technology faces as it expands into mainstream applications, particularly in sustainability and environmental governance. These issues limit the adoption, efficiency, and integration of blockchain solutions across industries and regions, raising concerns about their long-term viability and impact.

Scalability refers to a blockchain network's ability to handle a growing number of transactions without compromising speed or efficiency. Many blockchain systems, particularly those using PoW consensus mechanisms, suffer from limitations in transaction processing capacity. For example, Bitcoin processes only about 7 transactions per second, and Ethereum's original network handled roughly 30 transactions per second. In comparison, traditional payment systems like Visa can process thousands of transactions per second. This disparity creates bottlenecks as the demand for blockchain applications increases, leading to slower processing times and higher transaction fees during periods of network congestion.

Efforts to address scalability include the development of layer-2 solutions, such as the Lightning Network for Bitcoin and sidechains for Ethereum. These technologies handle transactions off-chain, reducing the burden on the main blockchain while ensuring security and accuracy. Additionally, alternative consensus mechanisms like PoS offer higher throughput and lower energy consumption, making them more scalable. However, implementing these solutions requires significant technical expertise, time, and investment, which can delay their adoption and effectiveness.

Regulatory hurdles further complicate the widespread adoption of blockchain technology. Governments and regulatory bodies are still grappling with how to classify and govern blockchain-based applications, including cryptocurrencies, smart contracts, and decentralized finance (DeFi). The lack of consistent regulations across countries creates uncertainty for businesses and investors, hindering innovation and adoption.

One of the main regulatory concerns is the potential for blockchain to facilitate illegal activities, such as money laundering, fraud, and tax evasion. The pseudonymous nature of many blockchain transactions makes it challenging for authorities to trace illicit activities, prompting calls for stricter regulations. Governments have introduced measures such as anti-money laundering (AML) and know-your-customer (KYC) requirements to address these concerns. However, implementing these measures can be technically and administratively complex, particularly for decentralized platforms that lack a central authority.

Data privacy regulations, such as the General Data Protection Regulation (GDPR) in the European Union, also present challenges for blockchain adoption. Blockchain's immutable nature conflicts with the GDPR's "right to be forgotten," which allows individuals to request the deletion of their personal data. Reconciling these requirements with blockchain's design requires innovative solutions, such as zero-knowledge proofs or private blockchains, but these approaches can introduce additional complexity and cost.

Cross-border regulatory disparities further hinder blockchain adoption. For instance, a project operating in multiple jurisdictions may face conflicting rules regarding data storage, taxation, and compliance. This inconsistency creates barriers for global-scale implementations and discourages investment in blockchain technologies.

Addressing scalability and regulatory hurdles is essential for blockchain to achieve its full potential. While technological innovations and evolving regulations are making progress, overcoming these challenges remains a critical priority for the future of blockchain applications in sustainability and beyond.

Chapter 5: Green Technologies in Various Industries

Green technologies are transforming industries worldwide, offering innovative solutions to reduce environmental impact, enhance resource efficiency, and drive sustainable growth. From manufacturing and construction to transportation and agriculture, these technologies are reshaping traditional practices and enabling businesses to align with sustainability goals. This chapter explores the application of green technologies across key industries, highlighting their role in reducing emissions, conserving resources, and fostering a more sustainable future. Through detailed insights, it examines how industries are integrating these innovations to address environmental challenges while maintaining economic viability.

Green Tech in Transportation

Green technology in transportation is revolutionizing the industry by reducing emissions, enhancing efficiency, and promoting sustainable mobility solutions.

Electrification of Vehicles

The electrification of vehicles is a transformative development in the transportation sector, aimed at reducing greenhouse gas emissions, improving energy efficiency, and decreasing reliance on fossil fuels. EVs, including battery electric vehicles (BEVs), plug-in hybrid electric vehicles (PHEVs), and fuel cell electric vehicles (FCEVs), are at the forefront of this transition, supported by advancements in battery technology, charging infrastructure, and policy incentives.

One of the key drivers of vehicle electrification is the development of high-performance batteries, particularly lithium-ion technology. Modern EV batteries offer higher energy densities, faster charging times, and longer lifespans than their predecessors. Innovations such as solid-state batteries and lithium-sulfur chemistries are further enhancing the efficiency and reliability of EVs, addressing concerns about range and charging speed. These advancements make EVs increasingly competitive with internal combustion engine (ICE) vehicles in terms of performance and convenience.

Charging infrastructure is another critical component of vehicle electrification. Governments and private companies are investing heavily in the deployment of public charging networks to support the growing number of EVs on the road. Fast-charging stations, which can replenish an EV's battery in minutes rather than hours, are becoming more widespread, alleviating range anxiety and encouraging adoption. Home charging solutions, powered by renewable energy sources like solar panels, further integrate EVs into sustainable energy systems.

The electrification of public transportation is a significant step toward sustainable urban mobility. Electric buses, trains, and trams are replacing traditional diesel-powered vehicles, reducing emissions and improving air quality in cities. Many governments are prioritizing the electrification of public fleets through subsidies and policy mandates, accelerating the transition to cleaner public transport systems.

Commercial and industrial vehicles are also undergoing electrification, driven by advancements in battery technology and the need to comply with stricter emissions regulations. Electric delivery vans, trucks, and construction equipment are becoming more prevalent, offering quieter and more energy-efficient alternatives to conventional vehicles. These innovations help companies reduce their carbon footprints while meeting growing consumer demand for sustainable practices.

Policy incentives play a crucial role in promoting the electrification of vehicles. Governments worldwide are implementing subsidies, tax credits, and grants to make EVs more affordable for consumers. Many regions are also setting ambitious targets for phasing out ICE vehicles, creating a regulatory environment that encourages the adoption of EVs. These policies are complemented by investments in research and development, which continue to drive innovation in the EV sector.

Electrification extends beyond individual vehicles to include advancements in infrastructure and grid integration. Vehicle-to-grid (V2G) technologies allow EVs to act as mobile energy storage units, feeding electricity back into the grid during peak demand. This integration supports the transition to renewable energy systems by stabilizing grids and enhancing energy resilience.

The electrification of vehicles represents a paradigm shift in the transportation sector, addressing environmental challenges while paving the way for sustainable mobility solutions. Through continuous innovation and collaboration among stakeholders, electrification is transforming how people and goods move, contributing to a cleaner and more efficient future.

Sustainable Aviation Technologies

Sustainable aviation technologies are reshaping the future of air travel by addressing the environmental challenges posed by traditional aviation. With the aviation industry accounting for a significant share of global greenhouse gas emissions, the development and adoption of innovative technologies are critical for reducing the sector's environmental impact while maintaining efficiency and connectivity.

One of the most promising advancements in sustainable aviation is the development of alternative fuels. Sustainable aviation fuels (SAFs), such as biofuels derived from renewable feedstocks like algae, waste oils, and agricultural residues, are gaining traction as a cleaner alternative to conventional jet fuel. SAFs can reduce lifecycle greenhouse gas emissions by up to 80%, depending on the feedstock and production process. As they are compatible with existing aircraft engines, SAFs offer a near-term solution for reducing emissions without requiring significant modifications to current fleets.

Electric and hybrid-electric propulsion systems represent another transformative technology in sustainable aviation. Electric aircraft, powered entirely by batteries, are being developed for short-haul flights, offering zero emissions during operation. Hybrid-electric systems, which combine conventional engines with electric motors, provide a transitional solution for longer flights by reducing fuel consumption and emissions. Advances in battery technology, including higher energy densities and lighter materials, are enabling the development of more efficient electric aircraft.

Hydrogen-powered aviation is emerging as a long-term solution for sustainable air travel. Hydrogen fuel cells generate electricity by combining hydrogen with oxygen, producing only water vapor as a byproduct. Aircraft powered by hydrogen fuel cells can achieve zero emissions while offering a high energy-to-weight ratio, making them suitable for medium and long-haul flights. Challenges such as hydrogen storage and infrastructure development are being actively addressed to enable broader adoption of this technology.

Aerodynamic improvements and lightweight materials are also contributing to sustainable aviation. Advanced wing designs, such as blended wing bodies and laminar flow wings, reduce drag and improve fuel efficiency. The use of lightweight composite materials in aircraft construction decreases overall weight, further enhancing energy efficiency and reducing emissions. These innovations not only lower fuel consumption but also improve the performance and range of modern aircraft.

Digital technologies are playing a critical role in optimizing flight operations for sustainability. AI-driven systems analyze real-time data to optimize flight paths, speeds, and altitudes, minimizing fuel use and emissions. Digital twin technology allows airlines to simulate and monitor aircraft performance, enabling predictive maintenance and reducing unnecessary fuel consumption. These tools enhance operational efficiency while reducing the carbon footprint of each flight.

Airport infrastructure is also evolving to support sustainable aviation. Renewable energy installations, such as solar panels and wind turbines, are powering airport operations, while electric ground vehicles reduce emissions from ground support equipment. Innovations in air traffic management, such as satellite-based navigation systems, help reduce delays and fuel use by optimizing flight scheduling and routing.

Sustainable aviation technologies represent a comprehensive effort to transform the aviation industry into a cleaner and more efficient sector. By integrating alternative fuels, advanced propulsion systems, aerodynamic designs, and digital tools, the industry is taking significant steps toward achieving long-term environmental sustainability.

Smart City Transportation Systems

Smart city transportation systems are transforming urban mobility by integrating advanced technologies to create efficient, sustainable, and user-centric transport networks. These systems aim to reduce congestion, minimize environmental impact, and improve accessibility by leveraging digital solutions, data analytics, and innovative infrastructure.

One of the core components of smart city transportation systems is intelligent traffic management. Advanced traffic monitoring tools, such as sensors, cameras, and IoT devices, collect real-time data on traffic flow, congestion hotspots, and accidents. This data is analyzed using AI to optimize traffic signal timings, reroute vehicles, and predict congestion patterns. Dynamic traffic management systems enable cities to respond to changing conditions in real time, reducing delays and fuel consumption while enhancing overall efficiency.

Public transportation is a key focus of smart city initiatives. Modern transit systems are incorporating real-time tracking and mobile applications to provide passengers with up-to-date information on schedules, delays, and routes. Smart ticketing systems, such as contactless payments and mobile apps, streamline the boarding process and improve convenience. Additionally, electric and autonomous buses are being introduced to reduce emissions and enhance safety, marking a significant shift toward greener and more efficient public transit.

Shared mobility services, including ride-sharing, bike-sharing, and e-scooter programs, are integral to smart city transportation systems. These services use digital platforms to match users with vehicles, promoting the efficient use of resources and reducing the number of private vehicles on the road. Shared mobility options also integrate seamlessly with public transit networks, enabling multimodal travel and expanding access to affordable, sustainable transportation.

EVs play a crucial role in smart city transportation, supported by extensive charging infrastructure and energy management systems. Smart grids and V2G technologies enable EVs to interact with the energy system, charging during periods of low demand and feeding energy back into the grid when needed. This integration enhances energy resilience while reducing the carbon footprint of urban mobility.

Autonomous vehicles (AVs) are another transformative element of smart city transportation. AVs use sensors, AI, and connectivity to navigate and operate without human intervention, offering the potential for safer and more efficient transportation. In smart cities, autonomous shuttles and taxis are being tested to provide on-demand mobility services, reduce congestion, and improve accessibility for people with disabilities or limited mobility.

Sustainability is a central goal of smart city transportation systems. Infrastructure such as dedicated bike lanes, pedestrian-friendly zones, and integrated transit hubs encourages active and low-carbon modes of travel. Renewable energy sources, such as solar-powered bus shelters and EV charging stations, further reduce the environmental impact of urban mobility.

Data-driven decision-making is fundamental to the success of smart city transportation systems. Urban planners and policymakers rely on analytics to evaluate the performance of transportation networks, identify inefficiencies, and develop targeted interventions. Real-time data sharing between government agencies, service providers, and users ensures that transportation systems remain adaptive and responsive to the needs of growing urban populations.

By integrating cutting-edge technologies and sustainable practices, smart city transportation systems are redefining urban mobility. These systems prioritize efficiency, accessibility, and environmental stewardship, paving the way for more connected, livable, and sustainable cities.

Circular Economy and Green Tech

Circular economy and green technology work hand in hand to minimize waste, optimize resource use, and drive sustainable economic growth.

Waste-to-Resource Innovations

Waste-to-resource innovations are transforming the way societies manage waste by turning discarded materials into valuable resources, contributing to the principles of a circular economy. These technologies and processes not only reduce environmental pollution but also conserve natural resources, reduce greenhouse gas emissions, and create economic opportunities.

One of the most prominent waste-to-resource innovations is waste-to-energy (WTE) technology. This process involves converting non-recyclable waste into usable forms of energy, such as electricity, heat, or fuel. Incineration, gasification, and pyrolysis are common methods used in WTE facilities. For example, municipal solid waste is incinerated to generate electricity, while gasification breaks down waste into syngas, which can be used to produce electricity or refined into fuels. These technologies divert waste from landfills and reduce methane emissions while recovering energy from materials that would otherwise go unused.

Biogas production is another key waste-to-resource innovation. Organic waste from agricultural operations, food processing, and households is decomposed in anaerobic digesters to produce biogas, a renewable energy source. The byproduct of this process, digestate, is rich in nutrients and can be used as a fertilizer, closing the loop between waste generation and agricultural production. Biogas systems not only provide a sustainable energy source but also reduce the volume of organic waste and its associated environmental impacts.

Recycling technologies are also advancing to recover valuable materials from complex waste streams. Innovations in chemical recycling, for example, allow plastics to be broken down into their molecular components and reprocessed into new materials. Unlike traditional mechanical recycling, which degrades the quality of plastics over time, chemical recycling produces high-quality outputs that can be reused indefinitely. Similarly, electronic waste recycling technologies recover precious metals, such as gold, silver, and palladium, from discarded devices, reducing the need for mining and preserving finite resources.

Wastewater treatment is being revolutionized by waste-to-resource innovations. Modern treatment plants are equipped with technologies to recover resources like phosphorus, nitrogen, and clean water from wastewater. Phosphorus, a critical nutrient for agriculture, is extracted from sewage sludge and processed into fertilizers, reducing reliance on mined phosphates. Additionally, energy-efficient processes generate biogas from organic matter in wastewater, turning treatment facilities into energy producers.

The construction industry is also embracing waste-to-resource solutions through the recycling and repurposing of building materials. Technologies that process demolition waste into aggregates for new construction projects reduce the need for virgin materials, lower costs, and minimize environmental degradation. Innovations such as 3D printing with recycled materials are further advancing sustainable practices in construction, enabling the efficient reuse of resources.

Industrial symbiosis is another emerging approach to waste-to-resource innovation. In this system, waste from one industry is used as raw material for another, creating closed-loop resource flows. For instance, heat generated by industrial processes can be captured and supplied to nearby facilities or communities, reducing energy waste and increasing efficiency.

By turning waste into valuable resources, these innovations are redefining the role of waste in the global economy. They support the transition to a circular economy by minimizing waste, conserving resources, and fostering sustainable practices across industries and communities.

Material Innovation for Sustainability

Material innovation is at the forefront of sustainability efforts, focusing on the development and adoption of materials that minimize environmental impact while maintaining or enhancing performance. These innovations address critical challenges such as resource scarcity, pollution, and waste, enabling industries to transition to more sustainable practices across production, construction, and manufacturing.

One significant area of material innovation is the development of biodegradable and compostable alternatives to traditional plastics. Conventional plastics, derived from fossil fuels, contribute to long-lasting environmental pollution and microplastic accumulation. Bioplastics, made from renewable sources like corn starch, sugarcane, and algae, offer a sustainable alternative. These materials decompose more easily in natural environments or industrial composting facilities, reducing the long-term impact of plastic waste. Innovations in bioplastics are also improving their strength, durability, and usability in various applications, from packaging to automotive components.

Another major focus is on recycled and upcycled materials. Recycling technologies have advanced to create high-quality materials from post-consumer and industrial waste. For instance, recycled plastics can now be processed into fabrics for clothing, while construction waste is being transformed into aggregates for new building materials. Upcycling, which adds value to waste materials, is also gaining traction, particularly in the fashion and design industries, where discarded items are repurposed into high-quality products. These approaches reduce the demand for virgin resources and minimize waste sent to landfills.

Renewable materials, such as bamboo, hemp, and mycelium, are being explored as sustainable alternatives to conventional materials in construction, packaging, and textiles. Bamboo, for example, grows rapidly and requires minimal inputs, making it an ideal replacement for timber in flooring, furniture, and building materials. Mycelium, the root structure of fungi, is being used to create biodegradable packaging and insulation materials. These renewable materials not only reduce resource depletion but also have lower carbon footprints compared to traditional materials.

Material innovation also extends to the development of lightweight and energy-efficient materials for transportation and construction. Advanced composites, such as carbon fiber-reinforced polymers and aerogels, are being used to create lightweight structures that reduce energy consumption in vehicles and buildings. These materials offer superior strength-to-weight ratios, enabling the production of fuel-efficient vehicles and energy-saving infrastructure. Innovations in concrete, such as low-carbon and self-healing concrete, are also addressing the environmental challenges associated with traditional construction materials.

In the electronics industry, material innovation is driving the creation of sustainable components. Researchers are developing alternatives to rare and finite materials like cobalt and lithium, which are commonly used in batteries and electronics. For example, sodium-ion batteries use abundant and inexpensive materials, reducing dependency on critical raw materials. Similarly, flexible and biodegradable electronics are being explored for applications in wearable devices and medical implants, reducing electronic waste.

Material innovation for sustainability is also advancing through the integration of circular economy principles. Designing materials for reuse, repair, and recyclability ensures that products remain in circulation longer and reduces the need for virgin resource extraction. By creating materials that align with these principles, industries are moving toward a more sustainable and resource-efficient future.

Through these advancements, material innovation is addressing global environmental challenges and enabling sustainable solutions across industries and applications.

Circular Supply Chain Systems

Circular supply chain systems represent a transformative approach to resource management, prioritizing sustainability by keeping materials in use for as long as possible through recycling, reuse, and regeneration. Unlike traditional linear supply chains, which follow a "take, make, dispose" model, circular systems are designed to minimize waste and maximize the value extracted from resources. This approach aligns with circular economy principles, promoting environmental stewardship and economic efficiency.

A key feature of circular supply chain systems is the integration of recycling and resource recovery at every stage of the supply chain. Manufacturers design products with end-of-life considerations, ensuring that materials can be easily disassembled and reprocessed. For example, electronic devices are increasingly being designed with modular components that can be replaced or recycled, reducing the need for raw material extraction. Recycling facilities use advanced technologies, such as chemical recycling and robotic sorting, to recover high-quality materials from waste, enabling their reintegration into production cycles.

Product life extension is another core element of circular supply chains. By designing durable and repairable products, companies extend the useful life of goods, reducing the frequency of replacement and the demand for new materials. Businesses also offer repair and refurbishment services, ensuring that used products are restored to a like-new condition. For instance, companies in the electronics and furniture industries now provide refurbishment programs that keep products in circulation and prevent premature disposal.

Reverse logistics is essential to the success of circular supply chains. This involves creating efficient systems for collecting used products, components, and materials from consumers and returning them to manufacturers or recycling facilities. Reverse logistics networks include collection points, transportation, and tracking systems that ensure materials are recovered in a timely and efficient manner. Digital technologies, such as blockchain and IoT, enhance transparency and accountability in reverse logistics, enabling companies to track materials throughout their lifecycle and ensure compliance with sustainability goals.

Shared ownership and leasing models are also gaining traction in circular supply chain systems. Rather than selling products outright, companies lease them to consumers, retaining ownership and responsibility for maintenance, upgrades, and end-of-life recycling. This model is common in industries such as electronics and automotive, where leasing arrangements ensure that products are returned to manufacturers for proper disposal or refurbishment. These systems incentivize companies to design products that are durable, upgradable, and recyclable, aligning profitability with sustainability.

Collaboration among stakeholders is critical for building circular supply chains. Businesses, governments, and consumers must work together to create policies, technologies, and behaviors that support circular practices. Governments can incentivize circularity through regulations, subsidies, and public-private partnerships, while businesses can invest in infrastructure and innovation to facilitate material recovery and reuse. Consumers play a vital role by participating in recycling programs and choosing products that align with circular economy principles.

Circular supply chain systems are reshaping the way resources are managed, reducing environmental impact while creating economic opportunities. By closing resource loops and prioritizing sustainable practices, these systems are driving a fundamental shift toward a more resilient and environmentally responsible global economy.

Innovations in Green Building Design

Innovations in green building design are revolutionizing construction practices by prioritizing energy efficiency, resource conservation, and environmental sustainability.

Smart Building Technologies

Smart building technologies are transforming the way buildings are designed, operated, and maintained, integrating advanced systems to enhance energy efficiency, comfort, and sustainability. By leveraging IoT devices, AI, and data analytics, smart buildings optimize resource usage, reduce operational costs, and minimize their environmental impact.

One of the core components of smart buildings is intelligent energy management systems. These systems monitor and control energy consumption in real time, optimizing the use of HVAC systems, lighting, and other building operations. IoT sensors collect data on occupancy, temperature, and natural light levels, allowing the system to adjust energy use dynamically. For instance, smart thermostats can regulate heating and cooling based on the presence of occupants, ensuring comfort while reducing energy waste.

Smart lighting systems are another key feature of smart buildings. These systems use motion detectors, daylight sensors, and timers to control lighting automatically, turning lights on or off based on occupancy or time of day. Advanced lighting technologies, such as LED fixtures integrated with IoT connectivity, allow for further customization and energy savings. Smart lighting not only improves energy efficiency but also enhances occupant comfort by providing optimal lighting conditions.

Predictive maintenance is a crucial aspect of smart building technologies. IoT sensors monitor the performance of building systems and equipment, detecting anomalies and potential issues before they escalate into failures. AI-driven analytics predict when maintenance is needed, reducing downtime and preventing costly repairs. For example, a smart HVAC system might alert facility managers to clean filters or replace components based on usage patterns and performance data. This proactive approach extends the lifespan of equipment and reduces waste.

Water management in smart buildings is also significantly enhanced through technology. Smart meters and leak detection systems monitor water usage and identify inefficiencies in real time. These systems can automatically shut off water supply in the event of a leak, preventing water waste and property damage. Additionally, advanced irrigation systems use weather data and soil moisture sensors to optimize water use in landscaping, conserving water while maintaining greenery.

Security and access control are integral to smart building technologies. IoT-enabled systems, such as facial recognition cameras, smart locks, and keyless entry systems, enhance building security while improving convenience for occupants. These systems can integrate with other smart technologies to create comprehensive building management solutions, such as restricting energy use in unoccupied areas or alerting facility managers to unauthorized access.

Integration with renewable energy sources is another hallmark of smart building technologies. Smart energy systems can manage onsite solar panels, wind turbines, or energy storage systems, optimizing the use of renewable energy. Surplus energy can be stored or fed back into the grid, supporting grid stability and reducing reliance on fossil fuels.

By providing real-time data and automated control over building operations, smart building technologies enable significant improvements in efficiency, sustainability, and occupant experience. As these technologies continue to evolve, they are playing a vital role in reducing the environmental impact of buildings and supporting the global transition to sustainable urban development.

Green Materials in Construction

Green materials in construction are revolutionizing the building industry by reducing environmental impact, enhancing energy efficiency, and promoting sustainability throughout the lifecycle of buildings. These materials are designed or sourced to minimize carbon emissions, conserve natural resources, and create healthier indoor environments, making them a cornerstone of modern sustainable construction practices.

One of the most widely used green materials in construction is bamboo, which serves as a versatile and eco-friendly alternative to traditional timber. Bamboo grows rapidly and requires minimal water and fertilizers, making it highly renewable. Its high strength-to-weight ratio makes it suitable for structural components, flooring, and decorative elements. Additionally, bamboo sequesters carbon during its growth, contributing to reduced greenhouse gas emissions in construction projects.

Recycled materials are another essential category of green materials. Recycled steel, for example, is widely used in construction for structural frameworks and reinforcements. It offers the same strength and durability as virgin steel while significantly reducing energy use and emissions associated with production. Similarly, recycled concrete aggregates are used in new concrete mixes, reducing the demand for virgin raw materials like sand and gravel and diverting construction waste from landfills.

Low-carbon concrete is an innovative green material that addresses the high carbon footprint of traditional concrete, which is largely attributed to cement production. Low-carbon alternatives, such as geopolymer concrete or concrete made with supplementary cementitious materials like fly ash and slag, reduce emissions while maintaining performance. These materials often use industrial byproducts, further promoting waste reduction and resource efficiency.

Cross-laminated timber (CLT) is gaining popularity as a sustainable alternative to steel and concrete in construction. CLT is made by layering and bonding pieces of timber in perpendicular directions, creating a strong and durable material suitable for load-bearing structures. Because it is made from wood, CLT stores carbon, helping to offset emissions. It also has a lower environmental footprint compared to traditional construction materials, both in terms of production energy and waste.

Insulation materials have seen significant advancements in green construction. Materials such as sheep's wool, cellulose made from recycled paper, and cork offer excellent thermal performance while being environmentally friendly. These natural insulation options are biodegradable, have low embodied energy, and contribute to improved indoor air quality by avoiding the use of synthetic chemicals found in conventional insulation.

Green roofing materials, such as cool roofs and green roof systems, are also transforming construction practices. Cool roofs are made from reflective materials that reduce heat absorption, lowering building temperatures and energy consumption for cooling. Green roofs, which incorporate vegetation, provide insulation, reduce urban heat islands, and improve air quality. Both options contribute to the overall sustainability of buildings.

Finally, paints, adhesives, and finishes are being reformulated to reduce volatile organic compounds (VOCs) and other harmful emissions. Low-VOC or VOC-free products improve indoor air quality and minimize health risks for occupants while maintaining durability and aesthetic appeal.

By incorporating green materials into construction projects, the building industry is advancing sustainability, reducing resource consumption, and mitigating environmental impacts. These materials are critical for creating energy-efficient, eco-friendly buildings that align with global sustainability goals.

Net-Zero and Carbon-Negative Buildings

Net-zero and carbon-negative buildings represent the forefront of sustainable construction, aiming to minimize or reverse their carbon footprint throughout their lifecycle. These buildings are designed to balance or exceed their carbon emissions by reducing energy consumption, utilizing renewable energy sources, and incorporating innovative carbon sequestration strategies. As global efforts to combat climate change intensify, net-zero and carbon-negative buildings have become critical components of the transition to a low-carbon future.

Net-zero buildings achieve a balance between the energy they consume and the energy they produce, primarily through the use of renewable energy systems. Solar panels are among the most commonly integrated technologies, capturing sunlight to generate electricity for onsite use. Wind turbines, geothermal systems, and other renewable sources further contribute to meeting energy needs sustainably. These buildings often incorporate energy storage solutions, such as batteries, to store excess energy for later use, ensuring a consistent energy supply even during periods of low renewable generation.

Energy efficiency is a cornerstone of net-zero building design. High-performance insulation, energy-efficient windows, and airtight construction minimize heat loss and reduce the need for heating and cooling. Advanced HVAC systems, often powered by renewable energy, further optimize energy use. Smart building technologies, including IoT-enabled devices and AI-driven energy management systems, enable real-time monitoring and optimization of energy consumption, ensuring maximum efficiency.

Carbon-negative buildings go a step further by actively removing more carbon dioxide from the atmosphere than they emit. This is achieved through a combination of energy efficiency, renewable energy generation, and carbon sequestration materials. Innovative materials, such as carbon-absorbing concrete and CLT, are used to capture and store carbon within the building's structure. These materials not only reduce emissions during construction but also contribute to long-term carbon storage.

Green roofs and living walls are additional features of carbon-negative buildings. These vegetative systems enhance insulation, improve air quality, and sequester carbon through photosynthesis. They also support biodiversity and reduce urban heat island effects, providing multiple environmental benefits. Similarly, carbon-negative buildings often incorporate landscaping strategies that include planting trees and restoring vegetation to further sequester carbon on the property.

Water conservation is another important aspect of net-zero and carbon-negative buildings. Features such as rainwater harvesting, greywater recycling, and low-flow fixtures reduce water consumption and the energy required for water heating. These systems integrate seamlessly with energy-efficient designs, contributing to the overall sustainability of the building.

Policy incentives and certifications play a significant role in advancing net-zero and carbon-negative building initiatives. Programs such as LEED (Leadership in Energy and Environmental Design) and certifications for Passive House design provide frameworks and benchmarks for achieving energy efficiency and sustainability goals. Many governments offer financial incentives, such as tax credits and grants, to encourage the construction of these buildings.

By integrating cutting-edge technologies, innovative materials, and sustainable practices, net-zero and carbon-negative buildings are setting new standards for environmental responsibility in the construction industry. These buildings not only mitigate the impact of climate change but also serve as a model for future urban development.

Consumer Green Technologies

Consumer green technologies are empowering individuals to adopt sustainable practices and reduce their environmental impact through innovative and energy-efficient solutions.

Eco-Friendly Appliances and Devices

Eco-friendly appliances and devices are revolutionizing the way households and businesses consume energy and resources, contributing significantly to sustainability goals. These technologies are designed to minimize energy consumption, reduce waste, and lower greenhouse gas emissions without compromising functionality or convenience.

Energy-efficient appliances, such as refrigerators, washing machines, and air conditioners, play a central role in reducing electricity usage. Many of these devices are rated under programs like ENERGY STAR, which certifies appliances that meet or exceed energy efficiency standards. Advanced features, such as smart thermostats and adaptive load sensors, enable these appliances to optimize their performance based on real-time conditions, further minimizing energy waste. For example, smart washing machines adjust water and detergent usage based on load size, saving resources while maintaining cleaning efficiency.

Renewable energy-powered devices, such as solar-powered chargers and lamps, are becoming increasingly popular among consumers. These devices utilize energy from the sun, reducing reliance on traditional power sources and lowering carbon footprints. Solar-powered outdoor lighting, for instance, provides illumination without drawing electricity from the grid, making it both environmentally friendly and cost-effective.

Water-saving appliances and fixtures, including low-flow showerheads, dual-flush toilets, and water-efficient dishwashers, are addressing the global challenge of water scarcity. These devices use advanced technologies to maintain performance while significantly reducing water usage, helping consumers conserve this critical resource.

Eco-friendly appliances and devices are also incorporating recyclable and biodegradable materials in their design, reducing their environmental impact at the end of their lifecycle. These innovations are empowering consumers to make sustainable choices and contribute to a greener future.

Promoting Sustainable Consumer Behavior

Promoting sustainable consumer behavior is essential to reducing environmental impact and fostering a culture of responsibility in everyday choices. By encouraging individuals to adopt practices that minimize resource consumption and waste, society can collectively move toward a more sustainable future. This shift requires a combination of education, incentives, and access to eco-friendly options.

One effective way to promote sustainable behavior is through education and awareness campaigns. By providing information about the environmental impact of certain products and lifestyles, consumers are empowered to make informed decisions. For example, campaigns highlighting the benefits of reducing single-use plastics or the advantages of energy-efficient appliances can inspire individuals to adopt more sustainable practices. Visual cues, such as labels indicating carbon footprints or water usage, further guide consumers toward eco-friendly products.

Incentives and rewards also play a crucial role in encouraging sustainable behavior. Governments and businesses can offer financial benefits, such as tax rebates for purchasing energy-efficient appliances or discounts for using reusable packaging. Loyalty programs that reward sustainable practices, like bringing reusable bags or participating in recycling initiatives, create positive reinforcement for environmentally conscious choices.

Access to sustainable alternatives is equally important. Consumers are more likely to adopt green behaviors when affordable, convenient, and eco-friendly options are available. Expanding the availability of products such as biodegradable packaging, renewable energy-powered devices, and locally sourced goods ensures that sustainable choices are accessible to all.

By combining education, incentives, and accessibility, efforts to promote sustainable consumer behavior can have a significant impact on reducing environmental harm and building a more sustainable society.

Chapter 6: Future Possibilities in Green Innovation

As the world confronts escalating environmental challenges, the potential for green innovation continues to grow, offering transformative solutions for a sustainable future. Emerging technologies and forward-thinking approaches are reshaping industries, creating opportunities to mitigate climate change, conserve resources, and enhance global resilience. This chapter explores the future possibilities in green innovation, focusing on breakthroughs in renewable energy, artificial intelligence, biotechnology, and circular economy systems. By examining these advancements, the chapter highlights how innovation can drive meaningful progress toward a sustainable and equitable future.

Emerging Technologies

Emerging technologies are revolutionizing sustainability by introducing innovative solutions to address environmental challenges and reshape industries.

Hydrogen Energy Systems

Hydrogen energy systems are emerging as a promising solution for achieving a low-carbon energy future. By utilizing hydrogen as a clean and versatile energy carrier, these systems have the potential to decarbonize various sectors, including transportation, industry, and power generation. Hydrogen's ability to produce energy with water as the only byproduct makes it a critical component in global efforts to reduce greenhouse gas emissions and transition to sustainable energy sources.

One of the primary applications of hydrogen energy systems is in transportation. Hydrogen fuel cells, which generate electricity by combining hydrogen and oxygen, power vehicles such as cars, buses, and trains. These vehicles produce zero emissions during operation, offering a cleaner alternative to internal combustion engines. Hydrogen fuel cell electric vehicles (FCEVs) also benefit from faster refueling times compared to battery electric vehicles, making them particularly suitable for long-haul transportation and heavy-duty applications.

In the industrial sector, hydrogen is being used as a clean substitute for fossil fuels in processes that require high heat or chemical reactions. For example, hydrogen can replace coal and natural gas in steel production, significantly reducing emissions in one of the most carbon-intensive industries. Similarly, hydrogen is being explored as a feedstock for producing ammonia and methanol, key components in fertilizers and chemicals, with lower environmental impact.

Hydrogen energy systems also play a crucial role in balancing renewable energy supply and demand. Surplus electricity generated by solar and wind power can be used to produce hydrogen through electrolysis, a process that splits water into hydrogen and oxygen using electricity. The hydrogen can then be stored and converted back into electricity when needed, providing a flexible and long-term energy storage solution. This integration of hydrogen and renewable energy enhances grid stability and ensures a consistent energy supply, even during periods of low renewable generation.

Decentralized hydrogen production is another promising aspect of hydrogen energy systems. Small-scale electrolysis units can be deployed near end-users, reducing the need for extensive transportation and distribution infrastructure. This approach enables localized energy solutions, particularly in remote or off-grid areas, and supports the development of resilient energy systems.

Challenges related to hydrogen energy systems include the need for infrastructure development and cost reduction. Hydrogen refueling stations, pipelines, and storage facilities are essential for widespread adoption, but their current availability is limited. Investments in infrastructure and technological advancements are critical to overcoming these barriers. Additionally, the production of green hydrogen, which uses renewable electricity for electrolysis, remains more expensive than producing hydrogen from fossil fuels. Scaling up green hydrogen production and increasing the efficiency of electrolysis technologies are key to making hydrogen energy systems more economically viable.

Despite these challenges, hydrogen energy systems offer immense potential to transform the global energy landscape. As investments in research, infrastructure, and production capacity grow, hydrogen is poised to become a cornerstone of sustainable energy strategies, enabling deep decarbonization across multiple sectors and contributing to a cleaner and more resilient energy future.

Fusion Energy Potential

Fusion energy represents one of the most promising solutions for achieving a sustainable and virtually limitless energy supply. By replicating the processes that power the sun, fusion offers the potential to produce massive amounts of energy without the long-lived radioactive waste or greenhouse gas emissions associated with traditional energy sources. This technology, while still in its developmental stages, could revolutionize the global energy landscape and play a critical role in addressing climate change and resource scarcity.

At its core, fusion energy is generated by combining light atomic nuclei, such as isotopes of hydrogen (deuterium and tritium), under extreme heat and pressure to form helium and release energy. This process is fundamentally different from nuclear fission, which splits heavy atomic nuclei and produces significant amounts of radioactive waste. Fusion's byproducts are much less harmful, consisting primarily of helium, an inert gas, and short-lived radioactive materials that decay rapidly.

The fuel for fusion energy, deuterium, and tritium, is abundant and widely available. Deuterium can be extracted from seawater, while tritium can be produced from lithium, a relatively common element.

This ensures a nearly unlimited fuel supply, making fusion a sustainable energy source capable of meeting the growing global demand for electricity without depleting natural resources.

One of the major advantages of fusion energy is its safety. Unlike fission reactors, fusion reactors do not carry the risk of meltdown because the reaction requires precise conditions to sustain itself. If these conditions are disrupted, the reaction naturally ceases, eliminating the risk of catastrophic failure. This inherent safety feature makes fusion an attractive option for large-scale energy production.

The International Thermonuclear Experimental Reactor (ITER), currently under construction in France, is the largest global effort to demonstrate the feasibility of fusion energy. ITER aims to produce more energy from fusion reactions than is required to initiate and sustain them, a critical milestone for the commercial viability of fusion. Other projects, such as private-sector initiatives and smaller experimental reactors, are also advancing fusion technologies, exploring innovative approaches like magnetic confinement and inertial confinement to achieve stable and efficient reactions.

Despite its immense potential, fusion energy faces significant challenges, primarily related to the technical complexity and cost of achieving and maintaining the extreme conditions required for fusion. Temperatures exceeding 100 million degrees Celsius, higher than the core of the sun, are necessary to sustain the reaction, requiring advanced materials and engineering solutions. Additionally, current fusion reactors consume more energy than they produce, posing a major obstacle to achieving net energy gain.

However, ongoing advancements in plasma physics, superconducting magnets, and materials science are steadily addressing these challenges. Governments, research institutions, and private companies are investing heavily in fusion research, aiming to unlock its full potential.

If successfully developed, fusion energy could become a cornerstone of the global energy mix, providing a clean, safe, and sustainable alternative to fossil fuels. Its potential to deliver abundant and carbon-free energy makes fusion a transformative technology with the capacity to meet the world's energy needs while preserving the environment for future generations.

Scaling Innovations for Global Impact

Scaling innovations for global impact involves expanding groundbreaking technologies and solutions to address large-scale environmental, social, and economic challenges.

Challenges in Scaling Green Technologies

Scaling green technologies presents numerous challenges that must be addressed to fully realize their potential in mitigating climate change, reducing environmental impact, and fostering sustainability. While these technologies hold promise, several barriers hinder their widespread adoption, including financial constraints, regulatory obstacles, technological limitations, and societal acceptance. Overcoming these challenges is crucial for accelerating the transition to a sustainable global economy.

One of the primary challenges in scaling green technologies is the high upfront costs associated with research, development, and deployment. Many green technologies, such as renewable energy systems, EVs, and energy-efficient infrastructure, require significant initial investment in infrastructure, manufacturing, and installation. These costs can be prohibitive, particularly for developing countries or smaller businesses. While the long-term economic benefits of green technologies, such as reduced energy costs and improved efficiency, are clear, securing the necessary funding for large-scale projects remains a significant challenge. Governments, private investors, and financial institutions must collaborate to provide the capital required for scaling green technologies and making them accessible to a wider range of stakeholders.

Regulatory frameworks and policies also pose significant barriers to scaling green technologies. In many regions, existing regulations are outdated or inadequate to accommodate new technologies. For example, the integration of renewable energy sources like solar and wind power into national grids requires updated grid infrastructure and policies that support decentralized energy generation. In some cases, subsidies for fossil fuels continue to dominate, making it harder for green technologies to compete on an equal footing. Governments must create supportive policies that incentivize innovation, reduce regulatory hurdles, and facilitate the seamless integration of green technologies into existing systems.

Technological limitations also present challenges in scaling green technologies. While many innovations have made significant strides, there are still limitations in efficiency, storage, and infrastructure. For instance, renewable energy technologies like solar and wind are intermittent, meaning that they do not produce energy consistently. Energy storage solutions, such as batteries, are essential for balancing supply and demand, but current battery technologies are expensive and have limited capacity. Advances in storage technologies and grid management are necessary to ensure that renewable energy can be stored and distributed reliably. Furthermore, the materials used in green technologies, such as rare earth metals in wind turbines and solar panels, can pose supply chain challenges and environmental concerns of their own.

Social acceptance and behavioral change are often overlooked but are critical factors in scaling green technologies. In many cases, consumers, businesses, and governments are hesitant to adopt new technologies due to a lack of awareness, understanding, or trust. The transition to green technologies may require changes in lifestyle, habits, and established practices, which can be met with resistance. Public education campaigns, transparent information about the benefits of green technologies, and demonstrations of successful implementation can help overcome these barriers and encourage wider acceptance.

Finally, the global nature of the challenges we face in scaling green technologies requires international cooperation and coordination. Climate change is a global issue that transcends borders, and solutions must be implemented on a global scale. However, differing economic conditions, political priorities, and infrastructure capacities create disparities in the adoption of green technologies between countries. To overcome these disparities, international collaboration, technology transfer, and the sharing of best practices are essential.

Scaling green technologies is essential for a sustainable future, but it requires overcoming significant barriers. Financial support, updated regulatory frameworks, technological innovation, societal acceptance, and international collaboration are key to unlocking the full potential of these transformative solutions. By addressing these challenges, we can accelerate the deployment of green technologies and drive the global transition to a low-carbon economy.

Collaboration Across Sectors

Collaboration across sectors is critical to achieving sustainability goals and driving the transition to a green economy. No single industry, government, or organization can address the complex challenges of climate change, resource depletion, and social inequality on its own. To accelerate progress, it is essential that stakeholders from different sectors, including government, business, civil society, and academia, work together in coordinated and innovative ways. This cross-sector collaboration fosters the exchange of ideas, shares expertise, and pools resources to create holistic solutions that address interconnected environmental, social, and economic issues.

One of the most important areas where collaboration across sectors is needed is in the development and implementation of green technologies. Green technologies, such as renewable energy, energy storage, and electric transportation, require expertise and input from a wide variety of sectors. Governments play a pivotal role in creating regulatory frameworks and providing financial incentives that make green technologies viable. Private companies, on the other hand, are essential in driving innovation, scaling up production, and bringing technologies to market. At the same time, research institutions and universities contribute critical scientific knowledge and technological breakthroughs that lay the foundation for new solutions. Collaboration between these sectors ensures that green technologies are not only technologically feasible but also economically viable and accessible to a wide range of consumers and industries.

Collaboration across sectors is also key to fostering sustainable supply chains. Businesses in various industries rely on raw materials, energy, and logistics to operate, and these processes can have significant environmental and social impacts. By collaborating with NGOs, local communities, and governments, companies can improve the sustainability of their supply chains. For example, companies can work with environmental organizations to ensure that their raw materials are sourced responsibly and that waste is minimized. Governments can provide incentives for companies to adopt sustainable practices, while local communities can offer valuable insights into how sustainable practices can be integrated into specific regions or industries. This multi-stakeholder approach ensures that businesses meet sustainability standards while benefiting the communities and ecosystems from which they source materials.

Public-private partnerships (PPPs) are a powerful mechanism for driving cross-sector collaboration. PPPs leverage the strengths of both the public and private sectors to address pressing issues such as climate change, energy access, and sustainable infrastructure. Governments can provide policy support, funding, and regulatory frameworks, while the private sector can bring innovation, investment, and operational expertise. A well-known example of a successful PPP is the collaboration between governments and renewable energy companies to develop large-scale solar and wind energy projects. These partnerships not only facilitate the transition to cleaner energy sources but also create jobs, boost economic growth, and reduce greenhouse gas emissions.

Collaboration across sectors is also crucial in addressing social and environmental justice issues. Sustainable development must take into account the needs and rights of marginalized communities who are often disproportionately affected by environmental degradation. By collaborating with NGOs, local governments, and affected communities, businesses can ensure that their sustainability efforts promote social equity and do not exacerbate existing inequalities. For example, partnerships between environmental organizations and local communities can help develop sustainable agriculture practices that preserve ecosystems while supporting local livelihoods. Such collaborations are essential for building a more just and inclusive green economy.

In addition to these tangible benefits, collaboration across sectors helps foster a culture of innovation. When diverse stakeholders come together, they bring different perspectives, expertise, and resources, sparking new ideas and approaches to solving complex sustainability challenges. Collaborative efforts can drive innovation in areas such as circular economy models, sustainable urban development, and climate adaptation strategies. The exchange of knowledge and experience accelerates the development of solutions that are more effective, scalable, and inclusive.

Ultimately, cross-sector collaboration is essential for achieving the ambitious sustainability goals set by international agreements like the Paris Agreement and the United Nations Sustainable Development Goals (SDGs). By working together, governments, businesses, civil society, and academia can create systemic change, developing solutions that are economically, socially, and environmentally sustainable. Through collaborative action, we can drive the transition to a more sustainable and equitable future for all.

Policies to Accelerate Adoption

Effective policies are crucial to accelerating the adoption of green technologies and practices across industries and regions. By providing clear frameworks, financial incentives, and regulatory support, governments can create environments where sustainable solutions are not only viable but also attractive to businesses and consumers. A combination of policy tools, from subsidies and tax incentives to regulatory standards and market-driven mechanisms, can stimulate innovation, investment, and widespread adoption of green technologies, paving the way for a low-carbon and resource-efficient economy.

One of the most important policy measures is the provision of financial incentives. Subsidies, tax credits, and grants can lower the initial costs of adopting green technologies, making them more accessible to businesses and consumers. For instance, tax credits for installing solar panels or purchasing EVs help offset the higher upfront costs, which can otherwise discourage adoption. Governments can also offer direct financial support for research and development (R&D) in areas such as renewable energy, energy storage, and carbon capture technologies. By funding innovation, these policies accelerate the commercialization of new technologies, making them available to a broader market.

Another key policy tool is setting regulatory standards and mandates that push industries to adopt more sustainable practices. Renewable energy standards or clean energy portfolio requirements, which mandate utilities to generate a certain percentage of energy from renewable sources, have been effective in driving the transition to clean energy. Similarly, vehicle emission standards and building codes that require energy-efficient designs and low-carbon materials can stimulate the adoption of green technologies. By establishing clear and enforceable targets, these regulations create market certainty and force industries to innovate and comply with sustainability goals.

Carbon pricing, through mechanisms such as carbon taxes or cap-and-trade systems, is an increasingly popular policy to accelerate the adoption of green technologies. By putting a price on carbon emissions, these policies create financial incentives for businesses to reduce their carbon footprint and invest in low-carbon alternatives. Carbon pricing makes fossil fuel-based technologies more expensive and less competitive compared to cleaner, renewable options. The revenue generated from carbon pricing can be reinvested into sustainable infrastructure projects or used to fund further R&D in green technologies, thus creating a feedback loop that accelerates innovation.

Incentives for green infrastructure development are also crucial to scaling sustainable solutions. Policies that promote the construction of energy-efficient buildings, public transit systems, and charging infrastructure for electric vehicles facilitate the widespread adoption of green technologies. For example, governments can provide incentives for the construction of energy-efficient homes or retrofit existing buildings with advanced insulation and energy-efficient appliances. Similarly, policies that support the installation of EV charging stations and the development of smart grids enable the growth of clean energy sectors and the integration of renewable energy into urban infrastructure.

Public-private partnerships (PPPs) are an effective mechanism for scaling green technologies. By combining the resources and expertise of both sectors, governments and businesses can address market gaps and foster innovation. PPPs can help fund large-scale projects such as offshore wind farms, smart cities, or waste-to-energy initiatives that would be difficult to finance through private capital alone. Through these partnerships, governments can de-risk investments and ensure that green technologies are deployed at scale while businesses contribute innovation and efficiency.

Education and outreach are also important policy tools in accelerating adoption. Policies that promote sustainability education at all levels can increase public awareness and demand for green products and services. By educating consumers and businesses about the benefits of green technologies, governments can foster a culture of sustainability that encourages wider adoption. In addition, providing access to information on best practices and successful case studies can help businesses understand how to implement green technologies cost-effectively.

Finally, international collaboration is essential to scaling green technologies globally. Global agreements, such as the Paris Agreement, can set collective goals for emissions reductions and provide a framework for sharing technology and knowledge between countries. Developed nations can provide financial and technological support to developing countries to help them leapfrog to cleaner technologies and build sustainable economies.

In conclusion, a robust policy framework that combines financial incentives, regulatory standards, market-driven mechanisms, and international collaboration is essential for accelerating the adoption of green technologies. By creating a supportive policy environment, governments can drive the transition to a sustainable, low-carbon economy, benefiting both businesses and consumers while addressing pressing environmental challenges.

Vision for a Sustainable Future

A vision for a sustainable future envisions a world where economic growth, environmental stewardship, and social equity are seamlessly integrated to create lasting prosperity for all.

Imagining a World Shaped by Green Innovation

A world shaped by green innovation is one where sustainability is woven into every facet of life, from the way we produce energy to how we manage resources and design cities. In this future, green technologies and sustainable practices are not just alternatives but have become the mainstream, transforming industries, communities, and economies. The world we imagine is one where the health of the planet is prioritized alongside human development, ensuring a cleaner, more equitable, and prosperous future for generations to come.

In this world, the energy sector is powered predominantly by renewable sources such as solar, wind, and geothermal energy. Fossil fuels, once the backbone of global energy systems, have been phased out, replaced by decentralized energy grids that harness the power of natural resources. Homes, businesses, and transportation systems are all powered by renewable energy, dramatically reducing carbon emissions and mitigating the effects of climate change. Smart grids and energy storage systems ensure that energy is used efficiently, with excess energy from solar panels and wind turbines being stored or redistributed as needed.

Transportation in this future is green, sustainable, and accessible. EVs dominate the roads, with infrastructure in place to support their widespread use. Public transport systems are electrified and efficient, reducing congestion and pollution in urban areas. In some cities, autonomous electric vehicles provide seamless, on-demand mobility, reducing the need for private car ownership and cutting emissions. Cycling and walking are the preferred modes of transport in urban centers, where pedestrian-friendly infrastructure and green spaces are abundant. Furthermore, aviation and shipping industries have embraced hydrogen and sustainable aviation fuels, drastically cutting their environmental impact.

Cities themselves are transformed into sustainable hubs where green design principles govern every building and infrastructure project. High-rise buildings are constructed with eco-friendly materials like cross-laminated timber and energy-efficient designs that minimize resource consumption. Rooftop gardens, green walls, and vertical farming systems help cities combat air pollution, reduce the urban heat island effect, and provide fresh produce for local residents. Waste management systems are integrated into the urban fabric, with zero-waste goals realized through composting, recycling, and the reuse of materials. Circular economy practices dominate, ensuring that products and materials are reused, repaired, and recycled rather than disposed of.

The agricultural industry, once a major contributor to deforestation, greenhouse gas emissions, and resource depletion, has undergone a revolution thanks to green innovation. Vertical farming and precision agriculture have made food production more efficient and less dependent on harmful chemicals and excessive land use. Soil health is restored through regenerative agricultural practices, and synthetic fertilizers are largely replaced with organic alternatives. Technologies such as plant-based proteins and lab-grown meats have reduced the environmental footprint of food production, ensuring that global food demand is met without further degrading the planet's ecosystems.

Water management systems are similarly transformed. Desalination technologies powered by renewable energy are providing clean drinking water to communities facing water scarcity. Water-efficient irrigation systems in agriculture and smart water meters in homes and businesses help conserve this precious resource. In a world shaped by green innovation, every drop of water is used wisely, ensuring its availability for future generations.

At the heart of this world lies a deep commitment to social equity and inclusion. Green innovation is not just about environmental benefits but also about creating a more just and equitable world. Communities around the world have access to affordable, clean energy, and green technologies are accessible to all, regardless of socioeconomic status. Jobs in renewable energy, sustainable agriculture, and green manufacturing provide economic opportunities for people in every part of the globe. Education systems emphasize sustainability and environmental stewardship, ensuring that future generations are equipped to continue the work of preserving the planet.

In a world shaped by green innovation, the economy is no longer driven by the depletion of natural resources or environmental degradation but by the creation of sustainable value. Businesses focus on long-term environmental, social, and economic sustainability, and industries collaborate to solve global challenges such as climate change, biodiversity loss, and resource scarcity. Green innovation has transformed not only the technologies we use but also the way we think about growth, success, and our relationship with the Earth.

This vision of a world shaped by green innovation is one of hope, where technological advancements work in harmony with nature to create a better quality of life for all. It is a future where human ingenuity and environmental stewardship are aligned, leading to a prosperous, sustainable, and resilient planet.

Call to Action for Stakeholders

The time to act is now. As the world faces unprecedented environmental challenges—climate change, resource depletion, and biodiversity loss—every stakeholder, from governments and businesses to civil society and individuals, has a vital role to play in shaping a sustainable future. We must act with urgency, leveraging the power of green innovation to transition to a low-carbon economy, promote social equity, and preserve the planet for future generations. This call to action is directed to all sectors, urging collaboration, commitment, and leadership to drive meaningful change.

Governments have the responsibility to create the regulatory and policy frameworks that foster green innovation. It is essential to develop and enforce ambitious climate policies that promote renewable energy adoption, energy efficiency, sustainable agriculture, and waste reduction. Governments must invest in green infrastructure, such as clean public transportation systems, smart grids, and water management technologies, while incentivizing green technologies with subsidies, tax breaks, and grants. Strong, consistent policies that support sustainable industries will provide the necessary environment for innovation to thrive. Governments must also collaborate on the global stage, ensuring that climate agreements, such as the Paris Agreement, are implemented and that developing countries are supported in their transition to sustainable practices.

For businesses, the need for leadership in sustainability is greater than ever. Companies must embed sustainability into their core business strategies, ensuring that their products, services, and supply chains are environmentally responsible and socially equitable. This includes adopting circular economy principles, investing in green technologies, and reducing carbon footprints across operations. Companies that fail to act will risk falling behind in a rapidly changing marketplace as consumers and investors increasingly prioritize sustainability. Businesses should also work with other stakeholders—governments, NGOs, and communities—to co-create solutions that address global challenges, such as climate change and inequality. Collaboration and innovation should be central to business strategies, ensuring that green innovation is scaled and accessible to all.

Civil society and NGOs play a crucial role in holding governments and businesses accountable and advocating for policies that prioritize environmental justice and equity. These organizations can help raise public awareness about the importance of sustainable practices and the impact of green innovation on communities, particularly vulnerable groups. Through grassroots movements, educational campaigns, and public advocacy, civil society can mobilize action on a large scale. NGOs can also provide technical expertise, research, and data that help guide policy decisions and inform the development of sustainable solutions.

The role of individuals cannot be overstated. Every consumer, worker, and citizen has a part to play in driving demand for sustainable products, services, and practices. By choosing eco-friendly products, reducing waste, and supporting companies that prioritize sustainability, individuals can contribute to the growth of green markets. Personal actions—such as reducing energy consumption, switching to renewable energy sources, or adopting sustainable transportation—collectively make a significant impact. Furthermore, individuals can hold their governments and employers accountable, advocating for policies and practices that protect the environment and promote sustainability.

Education and awareness are central to empowering all stakeholders to make informed decisions. It is crucial to provide the tools, knowledge, and resources that enable individuals, businesses, and governments to understand the importance of sustainability and how they can contribute. Governments, academic institutions, and businesses must invest in education systems that emphasize environmental literacy and sustainability. This will foster a new generation of innovators, leaders, and informed citizens who can continue to push for meaningful change.

In this transformative era, we cannot afford to wait. The actions we take today will determine the future of our planet. Governments, businesses, civil society, and individuals must come together to scale green innovation, build sustainable economies, and create a just and resilient world for all. It is time to take bold action, embrace sustainable solutions, and be the change that future generations will thank us for. Together, we can build a sustainable future that works for the planet and for people.

Conclusion and Key Insights

As we conclude this exploration of green innovation and its transformative potential, it is clear that the path toward a sustainable future is not only achievable but essential for the well-being of our planet and future generations. This chapter brings together the key insights from the preceding sections, summarizing the critical role of green technologies, policies, and collaborations in driving the global transition to a low-carbon, resource-efficient economy. By reflecting on the challenges, opportunities, and necessary actions, we aim to offer a comprehensive understanding of how stakeholders across sectors can contribute to this ongoing transformation, paving the way for a cleaner, more equitable, and resilient world.

Recap of Key Themes

This section recaps the key themes discussed throughout the book, highlighting the critical role of green innovation in shaping a sustainable future across industries, technologies, and policies.

Summary of Renewable Energy, AI, Blockchain, and Green Tech

Renewable energy, AI, blockchain, and green technologies are all integral to creating a sustainable, low-carbon future. These technologies, when combined, have the potential to revolutionize industries, reduce environmental impact, and accelerate the transition to a more sustainable global economy. Each of these areas contributes uniquely to addressing the challenges of climate change, resource depletion, and environmental degradation.

Renewable energy is at the heart of this transformation. Solar, wind, hydropower, geothermal, and biomass are rapidly becoming mainstream energy sources, offering cleaner alternatives to fossil fuels. Solar and wind power, in particular, have seen dramatic price declines, making them competitive with conventional energy sources in many parts of the world. The integration of renewable energy into national grids is enhanced by energy storage systems, which allow for the capture and use of excess power when demand is high. Technological innovations in grid management, such as smart grids and energy storage, are making renewable energy more reliable and accessible, ensuring a consistent energy supply even when the sun isn't shining or the wind isn't blowing.

AI plays a significant role in optimizing renewable energy systems and improving energy efficiency. AI-driven tools can analyze vast amounts of data to predict energy demand, manage supply from renewable sources, and optimize energy storage and distribution. AI can also improve the performance of renewable energy technologies, such as forecasting weather patterns for wind energy production or maximizing solar panel efficiency based on real-time data. Additionally, AI helps industries reduce energy consumption through automation, predictive maintenance, and the optimization of production processes, leading to greater energy efficiency in buildings, transportation, and manufacturing.

Blockchain technology is another key enabler of green innovation, particularly in areas like energy trading and supply chain transparency. Blockchain provides a secure, decentralized ledger for recording transactions, ensuring transparency and traceability. In renewable energy markets, blockchain facilitates peer-to-peer energy trading, enabling consumers to sell excess energy from solar panels or wind turbines directly to neighbors or local grids. This decentralization reduces reliance on traditional utilities and empowers individuals and businesses to take control of their energy use. Blockchain's transparency and immutability also enhance the accountability of supply chains, enabling companies to track the environmental impact of materials and products from production to end-of-life, ensuring sustainability and reducing waste.

Green technologies encompass a wide range of innovations aimed at reducing environmental impact and promoting sustainable practices. These include energy-efficient appliances, EVs, sustainable construction materials, and technologies for waste management and recycling. Innovations in green tech aim to reduce the consumption of natural resources, lower carbon emissions, and minimize waste through processes like recycling, reusing, and reducing. For instance, EVs help reduce reliance on fossil fuels by providing an alternative to conventional gasoline-powered vehicles, and energy-efficient appliances reduce household energy consumption, contributing to lower carbon footprints. In the building sector, green technologies such as smart building systems and sustainable construction materials help reduce energy use and improve environmental performance.

Together, renewable energy, AI, blockchain, and green technologies offer powerful tools to combat climate change and promote sustainability. These innovations are driving industries toward greener practices, enhancing energy efficiency, and creating new business models that prioritize environmental responsibility. The future of a sustainable, low-carbon economy depends on the continued development and integration of these technologies, as well as strong policy frameworks and collaboration across sectors. The synergy between these technologies holds immense promise for creating a more resilient, equitable, and sustainable world.

Contributions of Green Innovation to Sustainability

Green innovation plays a crucial role in advancing sustainability by addressing environmental challenges, improving resource efficiency, and fostering economic development that respects the planet's ecological boundaries. From renewable energy to eco-friendly technologies, green innovations are reshaping industries and helping societies transition toward a more sustainable future. These innovations contribute to sustainability in various ways, from reducing carbon emissions to promoting circular economies, ultimately driving positive change in both the environment and society.

One of the most significant contributions of green innovation to sustainability is the reduction of greenhouse gas emissions. Innovations in renewable energy, such as solar, wind, and hydropower, have provided cleaner alternatives to fossil fuels, which are the primary drivers of climate change. As the cost of renewable energy technologies continues to fall, they are becoming increasingly accessible and efficient. The shift from coal and natural gas to renewable energy sources is one of the most impactful ways to mitigate climate change. Additionally, green innovation in energy storage technologies, such as advanced batteries and smart grids, ensures that renewable energy can be reliably stored and distributed, even during periods of low generation, further reducing dependence on fossil fuels.

In the transportation sector, green innovation has led to the development of EVs, which have the potential to reduce carbon emissions, decrease air pollution, and reduce dependence on oil. As battery technology improves and charging infrastructure expands, EVs are becoming more affordable and practical for consumers. This shift not only helps reduce emissions from one of the largest contributors to global warming—transportation—but also fosters the development of a more sustainable and efficient transportation system.

Another contribution of green innovation is the promotion of energy efficiency across industries. Smart building technologies, energy-efficient appliances, and manufacturing processes are helping to reduce energy consumption while maintaining or improving productivity. For instance, energy-efficient lighting, heating, and cooling systems in buildings reduce electricity demand, lowering carbon footprints and reducing operational costs. In industrial settings, innovations such as precision manufacturing, waste heat recovery, and AI-driven energy management systems help minimize energy waste, making production processes more sustainable. These technologies enable businesses to reduce their environmental impact while increasing cost savings, creating a win-win situation for both the planet and the economy.

Circular economy principles are also a key aspect of green innovation. By shifting from a traditional linear economy—where products are made, used, and discarded—to a circular economy, where materials are continuously reused, recycled, or repurposed, green innovation promotes sustainability. Innovations in recycling technologies, such as chemical recycling and advanced sorting systems, enable materials to be reused more efficiently, reducing waste and conserving resources. Additionally, businesses are adopting circular business models that focus on product longevity, repairability, and end-of-life recycling. This shift to a circular economy helps reduce the demand for raw materials, decrease waste sent to landfills, and conserve natural resources, contributing to the long-term sustainability of ecosystems.

Green innovation also contributes to sustainability by supporting sustainable agriculture and food production. Precision farming techniques, which use data analytics, sensors, and AI to optimize crop yields, reduce water usage, and minimize pesticide use, are transforming the agricultural industry. Vertical farming and hydroponics are providing sustainable alternatives to traditional farming methods, reducing the need for large amounts of land, water, and chemical inputs. Innovations in plant-based and lab-grown foods are also helping to reduce the environmental impact of food production, offering more sustainable alternatives to traditional animal agriculture.

Furthermore, green innovation has the potential to improve social equity and quality of life. By developing affordable and accessible sustainable technologies, such as clean cooking solutions, renewable energy systems for off-grid communities, and affordable electric vehicles, green innovation can help alleviate energy poverty and improve living conditions for disadvantaged populations. It can also create jobs and stimulate economic growth in industries focused on sustainable development, helping to build a more resilient and equitable economy.

In conclusion, green innovation is at the forefront of driving sustainability in the 21st century. Its contributions span multiple sectors, from energy and transportation to agriculture and manufacturing, offering solutions that reduce environmental impact, conserve resources, and foster economic growth. As green technologies continue to evolve and scale, their role in creating a more sustainable, equitable, and resilient world becomes increasingly important.

Actionable Steps for Stakeholders

To accelerate the transition to a sustainable future, stakeholders across all sectors must take actionable steps, collaborating to implement green innovations and adopt sustainable practices.

For Policymakers

Policymakers play a crucial role in shaping the future of green innovation and driving the transition to a more sustainable economy. They are in a unique position to create the regulatory frameworks, incentives, and standards that will guide industries, businesses, and consumers toward adopting environmentally friendly practices and technologies. To accelerate the adoption of green innovations, policymakers must take decisive, forward-thinking actions that foster innovation, align economic incentives with sustainability goals, and ensure that the benefits of green technologies are accessible to all sectors of society.

One of the most important actions policymakers can take is to establish clear, ambitious climate and sustainability goals. These goals, such as reducing greenhouse gas emissions, increasing the share of renewable energy in national grids, and promoting sustainable resource use, provide a clear direction for industries and businesses. By setting long-term, measurable targets and implementing policies to achieve them, governments signal to the private sector that sustainability is a priority and incentivize innovation in green technologies. This can include binding emissions reduction targets, renewable energy mandates, and waste reduction goals that encourage companies to develop cleaner technologies and sustainable practices.

Incentives are another powerful tool for driving the adoption of green technologies. Policymakers can introduce financial incentives such as tax credits, grants, and subsidies for businesses and individuals who invest in clean energy, energy-efficient technologies, or sustainable infrastructure. For example, providing tax breaks for companies that install solar panels, purchase electric vehicles, or adopt circular economy practices reduces the financial barriers to implementing green technologies. Similarly, offering financial support for R&D in emerging green technologies ensures that new solutions can be brought to market quickly and cost-effectively. Policymakers can also support the development of financing mechanisms that make green technologies more affordable for smaller businesses and low-income communities.

Beyond financial incentives, effective regulatory frameworks are essential to ensuring that green innovations can thrive. Policymakers should develop regulations that not only promote green technologies but also phase out harmful practices. For instance, setting higher energy efficiency standards for buildings and appliances, implementing stricter emissions standards for industries, and encouraging the use of sustainable materials in construction can all have a profound impact on reducing environmental footprints. However, regulations must be flexible enough to allow for innovation and ensure that businesses are not unduly burdened by excessive red tape. Streamlined permitting processes for renewable energy projects, for example, can accelerate the deployment of green technologies while maintaining rigorous environmental standards.

Policymakers also need to focus on creating an enabling environment for green innovation through infrastructure development. Investment in renewable energy infrastructure, electric vehicle charging networks, and smart grids is necessary to ensure that green technologies can be integrated seamlessly into existing systems. This requires coordination between various levels of government, the private sector, and local communities. Policymakers should prioritize infrastructure projects that enhance the reliability and efficiency of renewable energy sources, making it easier for individuals and businesses to transition to sustainable energy solutions.

Moreover, policies that promote sustainable agriculture, forestry, and land use are critical to advancing environmental sustainability. By supporting practices that conserve soil, water, and biodiversity, policymakers can help reduce the environmental impact of agriculture and create resilience in the face of climate change. Encouraging the use of precision farming, agroforestry, and regenerative practices can reduce the carbon footprint of food production while increasing food security.

Finally, international collaboration and alignment are key to addressing global environmental challenges. Policymakers should work together across borders to develop international agreements that promote green innovation, share best practices, and create incentives for sustainable development. This can include technology transfer agreements, carbon pricing mechanisms, and international research collaborations aimed at accelerating the development and adoption of green technologies.

In conclusion, policymakers are essential to driving the green innovation agenda. By setting clear sustainability goals, providing financial incentives, implementing supportive regulations, investing in infrastructure, and fostering international collaboration, they can create an environment that accelerates the adoption of green technologies. The actions taken today by policymakers will have a lasting impact on the future of the planet, ensuring a cleaner, healthier, and more sustainable world for future generations.

For Industries and Businesses

Industries and businesses play a pivotal role in driving the transition toward a sustainable future by adopting green technologies, sustainable practices, and environmental innovations. Their actions not only contribute to environmental sustainability but also create long-term economic benefits, enhance brand value, and increase competitiveness in an increasingly eco-conscious market. To accelerate the adoption of green innovations, businesses must take proactive steps across their operations, from reducing carbon footprints to embracing circular economy models and integrating sustainable supply chains.

One of the most impactful actions businesses can take is to integrate sustainability into their core strategy. This involves setting clear, measurable sustainability goals, such as reducing greenhouse gas emissions, minimizing waste, and transitioning to renewable energy sources. These goals should be aligned with global sustainability frameworks, such as the United Nations SDGs, and provide a roadmap for how businesses can contribute to environmental protection while achieving economic growth. Developing a comprehensive sustainability strategy and embedding it into business operations helps companies not only meet regulatory requirements but also build resilience against future environmental and market risks.

Another key area where businesses can make a significant impact is through the adoption of renewable energy sources. Transitioning to renewable energy, such as solar, wind, and geothermal, helps businesses reduce their reliance on fossil fuels and lower carbon emissions. This transition can be facilitated by investing in on-site renewable energy generation, such as rooftop solar panels, or by purchasing renewable energy through power purchase agreements (PPAs). By integrating renewable energy into their operations, businesses can reduce their energy costs in the long term, improve energy security, and contribute to a cleaner energy grid.

In addition to adopting renewable energy, businesses should focus on energy efficiency across their operations. Implementing energy-efficient technologies, such as LED lighting, advanced HVAC systems, and energy-efficient machinery, can significantly reduce energy consumption. This not only lowers costs but also reduces the environmental impact of business activities. Businesses can also use data-driven tools, such as smart meters and energy management software, to monitor and optimize energy use in real-time, ensuring that energy consumption is minimized across all aspects of operations.

Embracing circular economy principles is another essential step for businesses committed to sustainability. The circular economy focuses on reducing waste, reusing materials, and recycling products to extend their lifecycle. Businesses can adopt circular practices by designing products for longevity, repairability, and recyclability. They can also implement take-back programs, where used products are collected and repurposed, reducing the need for raw materials and minimizing waste. For example, companies in the electronics and fashion industries can create closed-loop systems where old products are returned, refurbished, and resold, thus reducing their environmental footprint and creating new revenue streams.

Sustainable supply chains are also a critical aspect of business sustainability. Businesses should collaborate with suppliers who prioritize sustainability, ensuring that raw materials are sourced responsibly, products are produced with minimal environmental impact, and waste is minimized throughout the supply chain. This includes selecting suppliers who adhere to ethical labor practices, reduce emissions, and use eco-friendly materials. Businesses can work with their suppliers to improve resource efficiency, reduce water and energy consumption, and implement waste-reducing technologies. Sustainable sourcing not only reduces a business's environmental footprint but also strengthens relationships with consumers who are increasingly concerned about the sustainability of the products they purchase.

Innovation is central to scaling green technologies, and businesses should prioritize R&D in sustainable solutions. By investing in R&D, businesses can develop new, cleaner technologies and processes that improve efficiency and reduce environmental impact. This includes exploring sustainable materials, low-carbon manufacturing processes, and green product designs. Innovation in business practices also extends to adopting digital solutions, such as AI and blockchain, to optimize resource use, track environmental performance, and enhance transparency in sustainability efforts.

Finally, businesses must actively engage with their stakeholders, including employees, customers, investors, and communities, to build a culture of sustainability. Communicating sustainability goals and progress transparently can improve brand reputation, attract environmentally conscious consumers, and create stronger loyalty. Moreover, businesses can empower employees to participate in sustainability initiatives through training programs, green office practices, and incentives for adopting sustainable behaviors.

In conclusion, industries and businesses are essential drivers of green innovation and sustainability. By integrating renewable energy, embracing energy efficiency, adopting circular economy principles, and fostering sustainable supply chains, businesses can reduce their environmental impact, improve operational efficiency, and create a competitive edge in the marketplace. Through proactive engagement, innovation, and collaboration, businesses can play a pivotal role in achieving a sustainable future while generating long-term economic value. The actions businesses take today will shape the world for tomorrow, contributing to a cleaner, more sustainable global economy.

Final Thoughts on Green Innovation

Green innovation stands as a cornerstone of the global effort to combat climate change, offering transformative solutions that integrate sustainability into every aspect of society and industry.

Inspiring a Global Movement for Sustainability

Inspiring a global movement for sustainability requires a unified vision, collective action, and a commitment to transforming how we live, work, and consume. As environmental challenges become increasingly urgent, it is essential to foster a sense of shared responsibility among individuals, businesses, governments, and communities. This movement must transcend borders and encourage collaboration across all sectors to drive meaningful change that benefits the planet and future generations.

One of the key factors in inspiring this movement is education and awareness. By empowering individuals with knowledge about the impact of their actions and the benefits of sustainable choices, we can encourage a shift in behaviors toward more eco-friendly practices. Public awareness campaigns, community-based initiatives, and school curricula focused on environmental stewardship can help foster a culture of sustainability that becomes deeply ingrained in society.

Leadership also plays a critical role in inspiring change. Governments and businesses must set ambitious sustainability goals and lead by example, implementing policies and practices that prioritize environmental responsibility. At the same time, grassroots movements and organizations can spark local action, mobilizing people to adopt sustainable lifestyles and advocate for systemic change.

Technology and innovation can serve as powerful catalysts for this movement. By investing in green technologies and fostering innovation in renewable energy, waste management, and sustainable agriculture, we can accelerate the transition to a low-carbon economy. Moreover, partnerships between governments, businesses, and NGOs can amplify the impact of these innovations, ensuring they reach global communities and make a lasting difference.

Inspiring a global movement for sustainability is about building momentum, creating change at every level, and committing to a future where people and the planet thrive together.

The Role of Technology in Shaping the Future

Technology plays a transformative role in shaping the future, acting as a driving force behind innovation, economic growth, and societal progress. As we confront global challenges such as climate change, resource depletion, and inequality, technology provides the tools and solutions necessary to address these issues and create a more sustainable and equitable world.

In the context of sustainability, technological innovations have the power to revolutionize industries and transform how we produce energy, manage resources, and design urban environments. Renewable energy technologies, such as solar, wind, and geothermal, are leading the charge in reducing our dependence on fossil fuels, while energy storage systems and smart grids optimize energy use. In transportation, EVs and autonomous systems are reshaping how we move goods and people, reducing emissions and congestion while improving efficiency.

Digital technologies like AI, the IoT, and blockchain also play a critical role in shaping the future by enabling smarter decision-making, more efficient processes, and enhanced transparency. AI can optimize energy usage, predict climate patterns, and drive innovation in fields such as healthcare and agriculture. IoT devices allow for real-time monitoring of environmental conditions, enabling more effective resource management and waste reduction. Blockchain technology can create transparent, decentralized systems for supply chain management, ensuring sustainable practices from production to consumption.

The role of technology extends beyond solving environmental challenges—it also holds the potential to foster social and economic inclusivity. By providing access to information, improving healthcare delivery, and creating new economic opportunities, technology can empower communities and individuals worldwide. As we move forward, technology will continue to be a cornerstone in creating a more sustainable, equitable, and prosperous future for all.